A Student Guide to Japanese Sources in the Humanities

Michigan Papers in Japanese Studies, Number 24
Center for Japanese Studies
The University of Michigan

A Student Guide to Japanese Sources in the Humanities

Yasuko Makino
and
Masaei Saito

Center for Japanese Studies
The University of Michigan
Ann Arbor, Michigan, 1994

© 1994 Center for Japanese Studies, The University of Michigan, 108 Lane Hall, Ann Arbor, MI 48109-1290

All rights reserved

Library of Congress Cataloging-in-Publication Data

Makino, Yasuko.
    A Student guide to Japanese sources in the Humanities / Yasuko Makino and Masaei Saito.
        ix, 155p. 23cm.—(Michigan papers in Japanese studies : 24)
        Includes bibliographical references and index.
        ISBN 0-939512-64-5
        1. Japan—Bibliography. 2. Japan—Study and teaching—Handbooks, manuals, etc. I. Saitō, Masaei. II. Series.
Z3301.M32   1994
[DS806]
016.952—dc20   93-34031
                                                                                      CIP

The paper used in this publication meets the requirements of the ANSI Standard Z39.48-1984 (Permanence of Paper).

Printed in the United States of America

Contents

Preface	vii
Introduction	1
Chapter One: General Bibliographies	9
1. Western-Language Materials 9	
2. Japanese-Language Materials 16	
Chapter Two: Indexes	25
1. Periodical Index 25	
2. Newspaper Index 29	
Chapter Three: Publishers' Catalogs	32
1. Books 32	
2. Periodicals 36	
Chapter Four: Library Catalogs	39
1. Books 39	
2. Serials 42	
Chapter Five: Guides to Reference Tools	47
Chapter Six: Personal Names, Biographies, and Genealogies	52
1. Readings and Writings 55	
2. Who's Who 58	
3. Biographical Dictionaries 61	
4. Personal Name Indexes 65	
5. Biographies 68	
6. Genealogies 68	
7. Personal Bibliographies 69	
Chapter Seven: Dictionaries and Encyclopedias	76
1. *Kan-Wa Jiten* 76	
2. *Kokugo Jiten* 84	
3. Encyclopedias 92	
Chapter Eight: Gazetteers and Historical Atlases	98

CONTENTS

Chapter Nine: Calendars and Chronologies   104
   1. Calendars   104
   2. Chronologies   108
Chapter Ten: Japanese Literature   115
   1. Locating Individual Works   115
   2. Index to Poems and Parts of *Tanka*   120
   3. Translations   124
   4. History of Japanese Literature   126
   5. Dictionaries and Encyclopedias for Japanese Literature   126
   6. History of the Study of Japanese Literature   128
   7. Bibliographies of Research Materials   128
   8. Information on Individual Authors   130
   9. Acquiring Materials Found through Bibliographic Search   131
Chapter Eleven: Technicalities of Style   136
Chapter Twelve: Japanese Libraries and Research Institutions   140
Chapter Thirteen: A Final Note   142
Subject Index   146
Title Index   151

Preface

A quarter of a century has passed since the publication of Herschel Webb's excellent *Research in Japanese Sources: A Guide* by Columbia University Press in 1965. Since then, many convenient new types of reference works related to Japanese studies have been published. The present book, begun in 1983, is an update of the late Professor Webb's book. *A Student Guide to Japanese Sources in the Humanities* is intended to guide students who are about to start library research in order to prepare bibliographies for writing papers or dissertations, and to walk the students through the process of researching topics. We hope to make this task easier by teaching students an effective search strategy and by acquainting them with the appropriate, essential reference tools and bibliographies. This guide is also intended to be used as a textbook for a semester-long Japanese bibliography courses wherein the term project is the compilation of a bibliography on a particular topic. We have taught Japanese bibliography courses for many years at the University of Michigan and the University of Illinois at Urbana-Champaign, and we have used the earlier editions of the manuscript in classrooms in order to improve the content. We have tried to make this book readable, and even entertaining.

We have made it a point to be extremely selective choosing the reference works in this guide, including only the most important, essential, and representative reference tools published before 1992. We have used actual questions that we answered while working at the Asian libraries at our respective institutions as problems and quizzes in this book to make it more practical and useful.

These problems, generally placed at the beginning of chapters, are intended to draw the reader's attention to the type of reference works we will discuss in that chapter. We want the readers of this guide to stop and think about the problems with the help of hints that come at the end of each chapter, then proceed to read about the types of reference works available to solve specific types of problems. For each work, a description is given, including its strengths and weaknesses and its usefulness. We also explain what to use to supplement its limitations, if any. The quizzes can be used as homework when this book is used as a textbook, and they can give extra practice to those of you who would like a challenge. If you encounter any trouble, ask your teacher or an experienced librarian for help.

At the end of each chapter, the important reference works discussed there are listed to refresh the user's memory and to enable the user to identify types as well as names of reference works. For example, look at the chapter on personal names. We want to demonstrate that the reference works available as sources of information on people can be divided into several groups or types such as: reading of names, indexes of how to write names, directories or dictionaries for biographical information, and personal bibliographies that contain more detailed information. You can conduct a more effective bibliographic search by knowing the right type of reference works for your purpose. In other words, we want you to remember that individual reference works will undergo changes for various reasons, but if you remember the types of reference works available, you can always find newer works or other works by consulting guides to reference works. We also use a subject index, rather than repeating authors or editors in the general index.

Although we assume that the primary users of this book will be graduate students who are preparing to start their research, we expect that it will also be used by beginning librarians and scholars who deal with materials related to Japanese studies.

First of all, we would like to acknowledge Naomi Fukuda for her *Bibliography of Reference Works for Japanese Studies* published by the Center for Japanese Studies of the University of Michigan in 1979, and Emiko M. Moffitt, Deputy Curator of the East Asian Collection of the Hoover Institution, who invited both of us to serve on the Subcommittee on Japanese Materials, Committee on East Asian Libraries of the Association for Asian Studies, which she chaired between 1981 and 1984. She assigned us the task of updating Ms. Fukuda's bibliography, and during this time we came to know each other well enough to write this book jointly.

We would like to thank Weiying Wan, head of the Asia Library of the University of Michigan, and his staff, for their support. We would also like to thank the Department of Asian Languages and Cultures of the University of Michigan and the Center for East Asian and Pacific Studies of the University of Illinois at Urbana-Champaign for having given us the opportunity to teach our courses, and all the students who took those courses, who often inspired us.

We would like to extend our appreciation to the Japanese studies librarians who offered valuable suggestions for this book, particularly to Eugene Calvalho, East Asian Librarian at the University of Kansas, Mihoko Miki, Head of the Acquisition Division at the University of California, Los Angeles, and Frank Joseph Shulman of the University of Maryland, College Park.

A special note of gratitude goes to Eugene Wu of the Harvard-Yenching Library for his encouragement and for a travel grant to use its famed Japanese collection for the last check of recent reference books, to the Center for Japanese Studies of the University of Michigan for travel grants to use its excellent Japanese collection, and to the Research and Publications Committee of the University of Illinois at Urbana-Champaign for providing financial aid for final editing of the manuscript and preparation of illustrative matters. Our deepest, heart-felt appreciation goes to the unknown reader of our manuscript prior to publication, whose valuable comments and suggestions have added *garyō-tensei* 画竜点晴, the finishing touch, to make this work truly useful. Last, but not least, we would like to thank Professor Robert Danly, former Director of the Center for Japanese Studies of the University of Michigan; Bruce Willoughby, its Managing Editor; Elsie Orb, former Administrative Associate of the Center, and Karen Sansone, for her editorial assistance.

Yasuko Makino
Masaei Saito
August 1993

Introduction

In 1991 there were 42,345 new books published in Japan. In addition, approximately 30 to 35 percent of the books published previously are reprinted each year. According to the 1992 edition of *Shuppan nenkan* 出版年鑑, Japan ranks sixth in the world in the number of titles of books produced annually. Of the newly published books, 21 percent are on literature, 26 percent other humanities, 24 percent social sciences, and 16 percent natural science and technology. It is difficult to obtain the exact number of journal titles published, but the 1991 edition of the catalog of Japanese serial publications of the National Diet Library includes over 83,000 titles. *Nihon zasshi sōran* 日本雑誌総覧, 1988 edition, includes over 20,000 current titles. Out of this enormous number of publications, approximately 3,500 to 4,000 books and 1,500 to 2,000 serials have some bearing on Japanese studies.

It can be very difficult to acquire Japanese materials because of the extremely large number of publications, problems in the distribution of materials, and the lack of reasonably long exposure of new titles in bookstores. According to *Nihon shoseki sōmokuroku* there are over 5,850 publishers, 70 percent of which are located in Tokyo. The majority of Japanese publishers are small; one-third publish fewer than five books a year. The high rate of returns of titles from bookstores to the publishers means that new books stay in bookstores a maximum of six months.

Particularly troublesome is the acquisition of items published by various branches of central and local governmental bodies and academic institutions as well as local publications, which neither receive enough exposure nor are available in sufficient numbers because of budgetary constraints. Materials made available from the private sector also face the same problems. These materials cause difficulties for libraries outside of Japan in particular. Although there are approximately 400,000 titles currently available on the market, according to *Nihon shoseki sōmokuroku,* very limited numbers of titles are exported overseas.

HISTORY OF PRINTING IN JAPAN

The earliest extant, dated, printed work in the world is the *Hyakumantō darani* 百万塔陀羅尼,[1] or "mantras of the million stupas," manufactured and printed between A.D. 764 and 770 by the order of Empress Shōtoku. Most of the existing rolled texts are printed, although some were hand-written, and each *darani* is stored in a small wooden pagoda.

During the Heian period, many women authors flourished, and literary works, including tales and anthologies of poems, were circulated in books copied by hand, not printed. This tremendous amount of copying may be responsible for the existence of large numbers of variant editions, since it is easy to make mistakes and emendations during the copying.

Before the Edo period, printing was limited to Buddhist and Confucian books. But during the Japanese-Korean War in the 1590s, movable Chinese-character type and many printed books were brought back to Japan from Korea. At about the same time, movable alphabetical type and a printing machine, along with skilled printers, were introduced to Japan by an Italian Jesuit missionary, and the first so-called "Christian printing" using this machine was published in 1591. Although prior to the Edo period printing was not done for profit, during the Edo period large numbers of books were published. Literacy rates were raised because of the increased number of private elementary schools, called *terakoya* 寺小屋, for the commoner's children, as well as *hankō* 藩校, or fief schools, for the children of the samurai class. Thus, the market for books, particularly for the general

---

1. In 1966, a complete printed text of *Muku jōkō daranikyō* was found in Pulguksa, Kyung'ju, Korea. Korean scholars say it was printed in the early eighth century, which, if true, would make it the world's oldest existing printed material. See Kawase Kazuma, "Nihon ni okeru shahon to kanpon to no kankei" [The relationship of manuscript and printed books in Japan], a paper presented at the Annual Meeting of the Association for Asian Studies, San Francisco, April 1983.

Hyakumantō darani

public, increased. Books were printed by the hundreds and even thousands, compared to the one or two hundred copies usually produced earlier. Although books were published in the early Edo period using movable type, later books were printed using carved wooden blocks because of the expense and limitations of movable type. These carved wood blocks were much more durable and convenient for mass production, and were particularly well suited for the illustrations done by Japanese woodcarvers. This change in production method also contributed to the spread of the print culture throughout society. People also could borrow books from lending bookstores for a small fee rather than purchasing them. Publishers in Kyoto formed an official guild that had over 200 members by the 1720s. Bookstores in Edo formed private guilds between the 1620s and the 1640s and paid fees to receive protection from the government.

THE BEGINNING OF JAPANESE STUDIES

Although extensive records on early Japan appear in Chinese history books beginning in the first century (a reference to Japan in A.D. 57 appears in *Hou-Han shu* 後漢書 by Fan Ye [A.D. 398–445]), systematic study of Japan did not start in China. Marco Polo introduced Japan to the Western world at the very end of the thirteenth century, and with the coming of missionaries to Japan in the sixteenth century, Japanese studies began. The missionaries studied the Japanese language in order to spread the gospel and to teach their beliefs to the Japanese people. They printed books to teach the Japanese about Christianity and to teach the Japanese language to students studying to be missionaries. This latter type is the beginning of Japanese studies, in a sense. The missionaries sent reports and letters to their missions, families, and friends back home about their work, Japan, and its people. They also wrote travel accounts. They contributed a great deal to introducing Japanese culture to the Western world. As early as 1604 João Rodriguez, a Portuguese Jesuit priest who came to Japan in his early teens, wrote *Nihon bunten,* an extensive Japanese grammar book, as well as a Japanese-Portuguese dictionary that included 30,000 words. His and other Portuguese priests' works on Japan and the Japanese language were translated into French and read widely in Europe.

When the Tokugawa shogunate expelled the foreigners in 1639, only the Dutch and the Chinese were allowed to trade with Japan at Dejima, Nagasaki, but some of the scholars and physicians from other countries who stayed on there with the Dutch continued their studies of Japan. Some of their works were published in Europe in the early part of the eighteenth century and were read by intellectuals. Engelbert Kaempfer (1651–1716), a German physician, wrote *Geschichte und Beschreibung von Japan,* a book on Japanese history. In 1727 an English translation was published in London as *The History of Japan.* His original manuscript was not published in German until 1777, over sixty years after his death, but it was later translated into other Western languages and became a classic for Japanese history in Europe. Philipp Franz von Siebold (1796–1866), another German, also came to Dejima as a physician for the Dutch. He was suspected of being a spy when it was discovered that he had received maps of Japan from a government official, and he was thereby expelled from Japan. After going home, he published the first volume of the famous *Nippon:Archiv zur Beschreibung von Japan* in 1832. He contributed a great deal to the field of Japanese studies in Europe. By the early nineteenth century some research on Japanese language and literature had begun in European universities.

During the Meiji period, Japanese studies were carried out largely by British diplomats who were stationed in Japan: for example, Ernest Mason Satow (1843–1929), a Buddhist scholar; William George Aston (1841–1911), who wrote a literary history of Japan; and Sir George Bailey Sansom (1883–1965), a British diplomat who later became a Japanese historian and one of the founding fathers of Japanese studies in the West. Many American and European scholars and specialists who were hired by the Japanese government later contributed to the beginning of Japanese studies in their own countries. Erwin von Baelz (1849–1913), a physician; Adolph von Wenckstern (1862–1914), an economist; and Rudolph Lange (1850–1933), a linguist, are examples. Basil Hall Chamberlain (1850–1935), also British, came to Japan to study Japanese classics and later became a professor of Japanese linguistics at the Imperial University of Tokyo. He translated *Kojiki, the Record of the Ancient Matters* and authored *Things Japanese.*

Marius B. Jansen states in his extensive article, "The initial American interest in Japan was derivative and drew on published work by European traders," but "the Biddle (1846) and above all Perry (1853) expeditions to Japan brought a quickening of interest."[2] James Hepburn (1815–1911), an American missionary-physician who compiled and published a Japanese-English dictionary in 1867, devised a

---

2. "History of Japanese Studies in the United States," *Japanese Studies in the United States, Part 1* (Tokyo: Japan Foundation, 1988).

romanization system that is still the standard in this country. Other Americans who were employed by the Meiji government also contributed a great deal to the progress of Japanese studies. Ernest Francisco Fenollosa (1853–1908), a researcher in Oriental art, Edward Sylvester Morse (1838–1925), a zoologist, William Elliot Griffis (1843–1928), the author of *The Mikado's Empire* (1913), and Lafcadio Hearn (1850–1904), who authored many books and became a naturalized citizen of Japan, are a few examples of these *o-yatoi*, "government employees." Arthur David Waley (1889–1966), who translated Japanese literature, Noh dramas, and poetry, must be mentioned here, although he came a little later than the others. His translation of *The Tale of Genji* (1925–33), was particularly instrumental in making the Westerners acknowledge the existence of the great classical literature of Japan.

Though Japanese studies in the United States date back to the 1920s, many people who taught Japanese subjects during this period were laymen. A few who became the first generation of American Japanologists were Asakawa Kan'ichi, Hugh Borton, Edwin O. Reischauer, and Tsunoda Ryūsaku. In 1907, Asakawa Kan'ichi 朝河貫一 collected substantial numbers of Japanese books for the Library of Congress. By 1930, the Library of Congress, Harvard University, Columbia University, and the University of California, Berkeley, had Japanese book collections. Sakanishi Shiho 坂西志保 increased the Japanese collection of the Library of Congress during her tenure (1930–42) to 50,000 volumes, and it became the main source for Japanese studies during World War II. According to the report of the American Council of the Institute of Pacific Relations,[3] by 1935 two dozen universities and colleges offered some Japan-related courses, and eight offered some Japanese language courses. But the progress of Japanese studies in the early part of the twentieth century was slow and gradual.

Ironically, the establishment and the prosperity of Japanese studies owe a great deal to the Pacific War between the United States and Japan. During World War II, many young people in the United States received intensive training in the Japanese language for military purposes. Many of the second generation of Japanologists such as Marius Jansen, Donald Keene, Robert Ward, Edward Seidensticker,

3. American Council of the Institute of Pacific Relations, *Japanese Studies in the Universities and Colleges of the United States* (New York: Institute of Pacific Relations, 1935).

and Howard Hibbett came from this group. Another source for Japanologists were missionary children who were born in Japan. Edwin Reischauer and John W. Hall, for example, belong to this group. These second-generation Japanologists contributed to the remarkable growth of Japanese studies. After World War II, the occupation of Japan by the Allied Forces provided an atmosphere of interest in Japan, and many became Japanologists by abandoning their previous occupations. Japan's quick recovery from the ruins of war and its rapid economic growth in the 1960s also contributed to an interest in its language and culture.

A survey conducted by the Social Science Research Council under the direction of John W. Hall in 1970 found 408 Japan specialists working in 139 institutions, with 6,620 students studying the Japanese language.[4] This was a remarkable achievement considering the fact that there were virtually no Japanese studies in existence in the United States before the end of World War II. The second postwar survey of Japanese studies in the United States was conducted by CULCON (the Subcommittee on Japanese Studies of the U.S.-Japan Conference on Cultural and Educational Interchange). The *CULCON Report on Japanese Studies at Colleges and Universities in the United States in the Mid-70s* edited by Elizabeth and Joseph Massey appeared in 1977. Within several years, the number of Japan specialists doubled and the number of institutions offering Japanese studies increased to 196 (a 41 percent increase) while the number of students studying the Japanese language increased to 9,600 (a 45 percent increase). This growth came as the result of new sources of financial support for Japanese studies from the Japan Foundation, the Japan-U.S. Friendship Commission, and some Japanese corporations. The most recent survey, conducted in 1988 by the Japan Foundation, found 1,420 Japan specialists (1,224 in the United States and 196 in Canada), and approximately 25,000 college students studying the Japanese language in over 500 institutions. Another new trend in recent years is the increased interest of businesses and industries in Japan and the Japanese, which gives rise to the demand for specialists with master's degrees in Japanese studies or majors in business or law with a background in Japanese language and culture.

4. *Japanese Studies in the United States: A Report on the State of the Field, Present Resources and Future Needs* (New York: SSRC-ACLS Joint Committee on Japanese Studies, 1970).

As the interest in Japan grows, more and more books and journal and newspaper articles are being written. This tremendous increase of information on Japan in various sources necessitates a systematic bibliographic search technique for those who need to do research on subjects related to Japan.

Chapter One
General Bibliographies

Books that direct the users to information are called reference books and include bibliographies, indexes, catalogs, and dictionaries. **Bibliographies** are listings of independent bibliographic units arranged systematically and are usually used for finding materials in a given subject area or for selecting materials. Materials can be books, parts of books, journal articles, nonbook materials, and pamphlets. **Catalogs** show the location of the materials, which generally include books, journals, and other independent materials and do not include parts of books or articles in journals. **Indexes** are systematic listings of materials that would help a bibliographic search. The materials in indexes are likely to be smaller bibliographic units than books or journals. Usually each bibliographic entry in an index is a journal article or a portion of a book.

When using bibliographies, pay close attention to the coverage. Always keep the following questions in mind. Does the bibliography cover humanities only or both humanities and social sciences? If a bibliography is in a Western language and is published outside of Japan, does it also include publications written in Western languages and published in Japan? What types of materials does it include? Books only? Journal articles or portions of books? How about translations? Make it a habit to ask these questions before you use bibliographic tools. Particularly important is the coverage of the period.

1. WESTERN-LANGUAGE MATERIALS

Problem I-1. What should I use to find all the books on the history of Shinto written in English?

A bibliographical search has two sides: one is retrospective, namely, searching the materials written up until the present, and the other is becoming aware of current materials. Both are important aspects, particularly when you are about to launch a new research project, so that you do not duplicate someone else's effort. For a retrospective search it is essential to know the coverage of the particular bibliography. It is very important to know even with general bibliographies what subjects are covered and what are not. Problem 1 requires both types of search. Take special note of the fact that coverage of the period has to include the years before 1945, has to take the form of books, and has to be in English. Let us try and use the standard bibliographies to solve some problems.

Among the general bibliographies of Western-language materials on Japan, *Bibliographie japonaise* (I-1),[1] *Bibliography of the Japanese Empire* (I-2), *Bibliographie von Japan* (I-4), *Bulletin of Far Eastern Bibliography* (I-8), *Cumulative Bibliography of Asian Studies* (I-9), and *Bibliography of Asian Studies* (I-10) are essential for a retrospective, exhaustive search of available materials. The standard inclusive bibliography on Japan was started by Friedrich von Wenckstern, with the first publication of *Bibliography of the Japanese Empire* (I-2) in 1895. Wenckstern collected materials on Japan from books, journals, maps, and newspapers written in Western languages (excluding Russian) and published in Europe, in the United States, and in Japan. His work took Léon Pagès's *Bibliographie japonaise* (I-1), which covers the years 1477–1859, and extended it to 1893. Pagès wanted to show readers various aspects of Japanese life, such as culture, politics, constitutions, and foreign relations. It centered on Japanese history from a European viewpoint. Pagès's work, which consists of 658 items, cites mostly French materials; however, he collected works written in French, German, Italian, Latin, and Portuguese, along with some materials in English. The entries are arranged in chronological order of publication so the reader has to go through each entry. Fortunately, the bibliography is not very long.

With the publication of his second volume, Wenckstern extended the coverage of his bibliography to 1906. Although the amount of work involved precluded critical comments, some entries include brief descriptions, information on reprint editions, or contents. The book is divided into more than twenty subjects, covering not only the humanities and social sciences but also the natural sciences and

1. Full bibliographic information on the most important reference books is given at the end of each chapter.

industries. The arrangement is by format and type and differs from subject to subject, but individual entries are in alphabetical order by author, complete title, place of publication, number of volumes or pages, and year of publication. For periodicals, information on the table of contents in each issue with page numbers is included. The book also contains information on translations and various indexes.

Oskar Nachod continued Wenckstern's bibliography and extended its coverage from 1906 to 1926. German, English, and French were the major languages of publication in Nachod's compilation, but it also included works in Dutch, Italian, Spanish, Portuguese, and small numbers of Scandinavian and Slavic materials. Nachod changed the title to *Bibliographie von Japan* (I-4)[2] for the volumes covering 1927 through 1932. Both the Wenckstern and Nachod bibliographies included translations. Wolf Haenisch and Hans Praesent compiled volumes of *Bibliographie von Japan* (I-6) covering 1933 through 1937. The arrangement of this standard bibliography, as well as the language of the table of contents, changed slightly from compiler to compiler, and one can still use the text without really knowing the German language. Entries are numbered from Nachod's 1906–26 bibliography, even though the four volumes of *Bibliographie von Japan* continue Wenckstern's bibliography and extend its coverage to 1937.

Bulletin of Far Eastern Bibliography (I-8), edited by Earl H. Pritchard and published by the American Council of Learned Societies, covered the years 1936 to 1940 and closed the gap between *Bibliographie von Japan* and the cumulative edition of *Bibliography of Asian Studies,* which began in 1941. *Bulletin of Far Eastern Bibliography* originally appeared in five annual volumes of mimeographed issues and included journal articles on Japan, Korea, and other Far Eastern areas, as well as on China. It was eventually supplanted by the *Cumulative Bibliography of Asian Studies* (I-9), the first set of which covered 1941 to 1965, and the second, 1966 to 1970. This work contained both author bibliography and subject bibliography sections and included 170,000 entries. The author bibliography was

2. A new bibliography of works in German is in preparation: Wolfgang Hadamitzky and Marianne Kocks, *Japan Bibliographie: Verzeichnis deutschsprachiger japanbezogener Veroffentlichungen mit Standortnachweisen* (Munich: K. G. Saur, 1990–96), 6v. For finding bibliographies of materials in particular languages, consult chapter five, "Guide to Reference Tools."

arranged in alphabetical order and included all joint authors. When no author was cited, the citation was placed according to the first key word.

Bibliography of Asian Studies (I-10) is the most nearly complete annual bibliography. It aims to make available as complete a listing as possible of significant books and articles in European languages on Asian subjects. Unlike the Wenckstern volumes, this book covers only the humanities and social sciences. Besides books, many journals are systematically scanned for inclusion. After 1970, the bibliography is no longer cumulative, so each annual publication has to be used. The work is arranged first by general geographic area, then by country. Under the regions or countries, it is arranged by subject, which is further subdivided into more specific topics. The arrangement and coverage of subject areas have changed since the earlier bibliographies were compiled, so caution must be exercised not to miss information. Entries are numbered starting with the name of the author, title of the book or article, and the full bibliographic information. It is not the easiest bibliography to use because of its arrangement and because it is not cumulative after 1970, but it is the most comprehensive bibliography on Asia. Besides these standard general bibliographies on Japan, there are other selective and supplementary bibliographies such as *A Selected List of Books and Articles on Japan in English, French and German* compiled by Hugh Borton, Serge Elisséeff, and others. Borton's work is still somewhat useful because it is selective and includes important works up to 1950.

Unlike selective works such as Borton's, there are other works that were intended to be comprehensive. They are in most cases library catalogs, not comprehensive bibliographies in the strict sense of the word, but because of the nature of the holding institutions some of them come close to being comprehensive bibliographies. One such example is the Japan Foundation's extensive *Catalogue of Books in English on Japan 1945–1981*. Because of the nature of the library, its inclusion of 9,000 titles from National Diet Library (also known for this type of special collection), and its systematic inclusion of materials from the *Bibliography of Asian Studies,* it is quite valuable as a comprehensive bibliography of books on Japan in English. Although the Japan Foundation list is extensive, it contains materials written in English only, and for this reason one still needs to check the *Catalog of Materials on Japan in Western Languages in the National Diet*

Library Formerly in the Collection of the Ueno Library, 1872–1960, the *Catalog of Materials on Japan in Western Languages in the National Diet Library, 1948–1975,* and the *Catalog of Materials on Japan in Western Languages in the National Diet Library, 1976–1986.* These three works represent the books and pamphlets on Japan written or translated into Western languages collected by the libraries. The Japan Foundation's extensive catalog also covers broad subject areas.

Thus, the following bibliographies are the most important for a comprehensive bibliographic search of Western-language materials on Japan. The period covered by each of these standard bibliographies is as follows.

I-1. *Bibliographie japonaise* 1476–1859
I-2 & 3. *Bibliography of the Japanese Empire* 1859–1926
I-4 – I-7. *Bibliographie von Japan* 1927–37
I-8. *Bulletin of Far Eastern Bibliography* 1936–40
I-9. *Cumulative Bibliography of Asian Studies* 1941–70
I-10. *Bibliography of Asian Studies* 1956–

(Hint for Problem I-1: You need to conduct a thorough bibliographic search using all the bibliographies we have discussed so far because the problem includes pre-World War II materials and requires a systematic search. It is going to be time-consuming, and you need to be patient when conducting a thorough bibliographic search.)

Quiz. I-1. I would like to find books, written mainly in English, on Japanese festivals. I also know a little French and German.

Problem I-2. Is there any doctoral dissertation about higher education in Japan, excluding those written in Japanese?

For dissertations on Japan, check *Japan and Korea: An Annotated Bibliography of Doctoral Dissertations in Western Languages, 1877-1969* (I-12) by Frank Shulman. This annotated bibliography lists 2,077 titles of dissertations dealing in whole or in part with Japan between 1877 and 1969. Its twenty-four major subject areas, which include science and technology, are further subdivided and contain numerous cross-references. Within each subsection the arrangement is in chronological order by date of completion, and each numbered

14 CHAPTER ONE

entry lists the author's name, title of the dissertation, year, length, where the information was acquired, and a summary or annotation. Often, related publications are included. This comprehensive, interdisciplinary, annotated bibliography helps to identify research needs as well as informing students or researchers what has been done in their fields. *Doctoral Dissertations on Japan and Korea, 1969-1979: An Annotated Bibliography of Studies in Western Languages* (I-13) by the same compiler is a continuation. Both works have an index for authors, institutions arranged by country, and a biographical index for dissertations focusing on individuals. *Doctoral Dissertations on Asia: An Annotated Bibliographical Journal of Current International Research* (I-14), also compiled by Frank Shulman, should be consulted for more recent dissertations on Japan. Another helpful work is *Dissertation Abstracts International,* which first appeared in winter 1975 and is published semiannually. The latest information on dissertations can be found by searching the database of University Microfilm International. Thanks to Frank Shulman's tireless effort, dissertations on Japan in Western languages are well covered.

There is no way to conduct an exhaustive bibliographic search of master's theses, although there is a selective list of master's abstracts. Many institutions keep their own records, but many master's theses are unavailable since they are generally unpublished. A thorough retrospective search of *Japan and Korea* has to be done at an early stage of writing a thesis.

(Hint for Problem I-2: The key point is that you are looking for doctoral dissertations outside of Japan. Thus, bibliographies I-12, I-13, I-14, and recent issues of *Dissertation Abstracts International* have to be consulted to answer the problem fully.)

Quiz I-2. Is there any doctoral dissertation about Futabatei Shimei 二葉亭四迷 outside of Japan?

Problem I-3. Where should I go to find the major works on Japanese history for the year 1980?

In this problem you are seeking important works on a specific subject for a particular year. The languages of the works are not specified. After searching through the standard general bibliographies in Western languages, you need to do a similar search of materials written in Japanese. *An Introductory Bibliography for Japanese Studies* (I-15), published by the Japan Foundation and written in English, aims to provide information to non-Japanese researchers on scholarly works written and published in Japanese by Japanese scholars. It is convenient for nonnative researchers because it allows them to glance quickly over recent Japanese scholarship in their fields of specialization. It began publication in 1974, and each volume is published every other year. Part 1 covers the social sciences and Part 2 the humanities. Volume 1 covers publications within a four-year period, but the length of coverage of later volumes varies from two to five years. Each section is written by a specialist in the field, which makes the bibliography a great time-saver for researchers and students who are not fluent in reading Japanese. Since important works published during the years covered are selected by a top scholar in each field, this can be used also as a selective and evaluative bibliography. The details of arrangement vary from author to author, but generally bibliographic essays are followed by bibliographic notes. Different volumes do sometimes cover different subjects. For example, volume 5, part 2 (1980–82, published in 1987) covers Japanese history, archaeology, religion, intellectual history, language, literature, and art history. Volume 6, part 1 (1981–85, published in 1988) covers law, political science, international relations, economics, business administration, geography, cultural anthropology, and education. Business administration is a new subject to be included in this volume. The only shortcoming of this bibliography is that it tends not to be published promptly.

Problem I-4. Are there any recent translations into English of works on Japanese religions?

Although some of the retrospective bibliographies discussed above include translations and there are a few bibliographies of translations from Japanese into Western languages, the standard bibliography of translations is *Index translationum: International Bibliography of Translations* (I-11). It was published between 1932 and 1940 (nos. 1–31) as a quarterly publication, and after 1949 as a new series published annually. It is arranged in alphabetical order according to the French name for the country in which the translation was published. Entries are presented under the ten major headings of the Universal Decimal Classification System, are numbered under each division, and list complete bibliographical information including author, title of the translation, translator's name, place of publication, publisher, date of publication, pages, whether illustrated, and original language and title when available. Translations missed in previous volumes are picked up in later volumes. This publication is also very slow in appearing (for example, the 1983 edition was published in 1989).

(Hint for Problem I-4: First, define the exact year[s] implied in "recent" years, and also define the type of materials to be searched for, in this case, books. Then check recent issues of *Index translationum* and *An Introductory Bibliography for Japanese Studies*. In 1988 the Japan Foundation published *Catalogue of Books on Japan Translated from the Japanese into English*. In 1990, *Japanese Publications in Foreign Languages 1945–1990* [Tokyo: Nihon Shoseki Shuppan Kyōkai (Japan Publishers Association), 1990, 330p.] was published, which covers Japanese books translated into foreign languages between 1945 and early 1990; 5,250 items are included. For Japanese literature, *Japanese Literature in Foreign Languages 1945-1990* compiled by the Japan PEN [International Association of Poets, Playwrights, Editors, Essayists, and Novelists] is a very comprehensive source of this type of information.)

Quiz I-3. What are the recent translations into English of Japanese works on sociology?

2. JAPANESE-LANGUAGE MATERIALS

Problem I-5. I need to compare variant editions of *Nanbōroku* 南坊録. How many editions are known to exist? Are they published as facsimile editions? Is there any modern printing edition available?

Kokusho sōmokuroku 国書総目録 (I-16) and its supplement, *Kotenseki sōgō mokuroku* 古典籍総合目録 (I-17), are national union catalogs for Japanese books and manuscripts from the beginning of the country to 1867. They are owned by over 500 libraries and private collectors throughout Japan. *Kokusho sōmokuroku* is a comprehensive and extremely useful catalog of approximately 500,000 titles that were written, compiled, or translated by Japanese. It excludes works in nonbook formats such as documents. Arranged in Japanese syllabary order by title, each entry includes: reading of the title, numbers of volumes, category, title at head, alternate title, subject area, author or editor, date of publication or compilation, manuscripts or prints, name of the series when applicable, and name of the library or collection where the entry is housed. *Kokusho sōmokuroku* contains good cross-references.

There is a separate author index volume that can be used to find listings of each author's works. Entry is under the author's name and includes pseudonyms, title, date of composition or publication, number of volumes, and pages. The contents of over 970 monographic series, either manuscripts or printed or facsimile editions, are listed in volume 8. For books known to have existed by citation only, the source of this information is recorded. A revised edition was published in 1989-90. *Kotenseki sōgō mokuroku,* the first supplement, was published in 1990, and it includes 45,000 items, 10,000 of which did not appear in *Kokusho sōmokuroku.*

Since these extensive catalogs use many abbreviations in the entries, one must read *hanrei* 凡例 , or explanatory notes, listed at the beginning of each book, such as *sha* 写 (manuscript, hand-copied book), *katsu* 活 (printed book), *tō* 謄 (mimeographed material), and *fuku* 復 (facsimile reproduction). The Japanese word for variant edition is *ihon* 異本.

Kotenseki sōgō mokuroku has special marks of its own, which are explained in its *hanrei.*

If you read the example carefully, you should not have any problem in finding variant editions and modern printed editions under *ihon* and *katsu,* respectively.

(Hint for Problem I-5: The key to the solution of this problem is that you need to look for different editions of a work that was written before the Meiji era.)

Quiz I-4. I would like to compare variant editions of *Hōjōki* 方丈記. Are any of them printed in modern editions?

Quiz I-5. Is there a printed edition of *Tennōjiya kaiki* 天王寺屋会記? Is it the same as *Tsuda sōkyū chanoyu nikki* 津田宗及茶の湯日記?

18   CHAPTER ONE

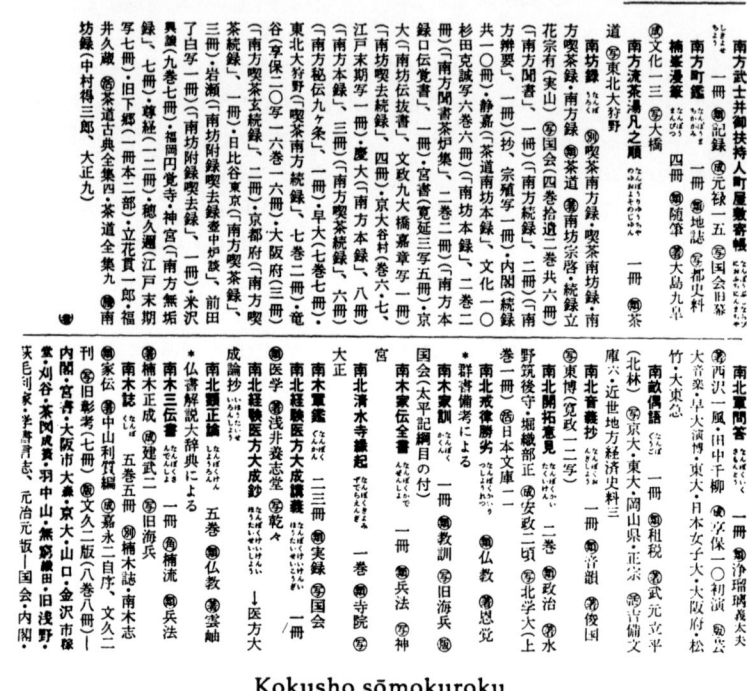

Kokusho sōmokuroku

(Hint: Important historical source materials are often annotated in encyclopedias as well.)

Problem I-6. I am looking for all the books ever published on *Hyakushuuta* 百首歌 by Sen no Rikyū 千利休.

The items we are going to discuss in this section are mostly library catalogs, which are not really meant to be general bibliographies. However, the Ministry of Internal Affairs of the prewar Japanese government required publishers by law (Shuppanhō) to send three copies of all publications to the ministry's office. Shuppanhō, or the Publishing Law, was especially effective because the penalty for offenders was severe. In addition, all books published in Japan must be sent to the National Diet Library (NDL) according to the National Diet Library Law. Because of these laws, items I-18 through I-24 in fact are national bibliographies as well as library catalogs. Since Japan is far behind the United States and some other European countries when it comes to inclusive, systematic bibliographies such as *Bibliography*

■南方且坐（写）久留米（二巻 二冊）（類）茶道 （著）宗朴 （成）宝永五
跋
南坊録 （別）喫茶南方録・南坊宗啓・続録立
方喫茶録・南方録 （類）茶道 （著）南坊宗啓・続録立
花実山（立花宗有） （写）新潟大佐野（「茶道南房
本録」二冊）（一冊）
城大菅（一冊） （類）伝記 （著）惜陰主人 （写）茨
■南木遺芳
南畝偶語 一冊 （類）租税 （著）武元北林
（武元立平）（写）茨城大菅（救餓大意と合「南畝
偶語」一冊）・閑谷学校（勧農策と合「勧農策
南畝偶語」二冊）
（版）南北顕正論 五巻 （類）仏教 （著）雲岫
（版）玉川大（上存 一冊）

Kotenseki sōgō mokuroku

of Asian Studies, which include both books and journal articles, we consider these library catalogs as the national bibliography, and use them as such.

Kokuritsu Kokkai Toshokan shozō Meijiki kankō tosho mokuroku 国立国会図書館所蔵明治期刊行図書目録 (I-18) is a classified list of approximately 120,000 titles published by Japanese, both in Japan and overseas, during the Meiji era. It is owned by the National Diet Library. Under each classification, arrangement is in Japanese syllabary order. Volume 5 contains a supplement and a list of Western-language books. Title, subtitle, alternate title, author, place of publication, publisher, date of publication, number of volumes, size, series, and call number are given for each work. Some entries include notes or tables of contents.

Teikoku Toshokan Wakan tosho shomei mokuroku 帝国図書館和漢図書書名目録 (I-19) covers Japanese and Chinese books acquired before March 1949 and is divided into seven sections. *Teikoku Toshokan Kokuritsu Toshokan Wakan tosho bunrui mokuroku* 帝国図書館国立図書館和漢図書分類目録 (I-20), covering the period from January 1941 to March 1949, includes supplementary materials. It was succeeded by *Kokuritsu Kokkai Toshokan zōsho mokuroku* 国立国会図書館蔵書目録 (I-21).

Zen Nihon shuppanbutsu sōmokuroku 全日本出版物総目録 (I-22), which covers the period from 1948 to 1976, and *Nihon zenkoku shoshi* 日本全国書誌 (I-23), its continuation, are comprehensive annual lists of monographs and journals published in Japan and added to the collection of the National Diet Library. The strength of these volumes is that they include both books and journals that are not offered for sale to the public, such as government publications and reports and publications of research institutes. The English title is *Japanese National Bibliography*. It is the national bibliography because all publishers are required by law to send at least one copy of each of their publications to the National Diet Library. Unfortunately, unlike the Library of Congress, which has a copyright registration program and a cataloging in publication (CIP) program that help to ensure that titles will be sent to the library, the National Diet Library has no such program and has been experiencing some difficulty enforcing this law and receiving copies of all publications, particularly local and not-for-sale *hibaihin* publications. *Nihon zenkoku shoshi shūkanban* 日本全国書誌週刊版 (I-24) is the weekly list of all the books, pamphlets, and serials processed by the National Diet Library during the week. It is divided into sections for government publications and nongovernment publications. Pamphlets and serial publications are listed separately in regular supplements. Each entry is numbered and includes title, author, place and date of publication, pagination and size, bibliographic information, reading of the title, and subjects. Quarterly indexes for titles and authors are published, and an annual cumulative edition of the indexes is also available. A cumulative J-BISC (Japan Biblio-Disc), a CD-ROM edition of Japan-MARC, is also available.

I-16, 17. *Kokusho sōmokuroku* plus *Kotenseki sōgō mokuroku* –1867
I-18. *Kokuritsu Kokkai Toshokan shozō Meijiki kankō tosho mokuroku* 1868–1912
I-19. *Teikoku Toshokan Wakan tosho shomei mokuroku* 1893–1940
I-20. *Teikoku Toshokan Kokuritsu Toshokan Wakan tosho bunrui mokuroku* 1941–49
I-21. *Kokuritsu Kokkai Toshokan zōsho mokuroku* 1948–90

I-22. *Zen Nihon shuppanbutsu sōmokuroku* 1948–76
I-23. *Nihon zenkoku shoshi* 1977–
I-24. *Nihon zenkoku shoshi shūkanban* 1981–

(Hint for Problem I-6: The question asks about books published up to now, which includes old books as well as recent ones.)

Quiz I-6. I have heard that Suzuki Takao 鈴木孝夫 published a book titled *Nihongo to gaikokugo* 日本語と外国語. Where can I find full information on this book?

(Hint: If you have no information on the publication date, what do you do first?)

Problem I-7. Is there a doctoral dissertation on the tea ceremony or related topics written in Japanese?

The meaning of a doctorate in Japan, particularly in the field of the humanities, is very different from that in the United States. In the United States, a Ph.D. is a certificate of demonstrated ability as a researcher, a passport to the academic world. On the other hand, in Japan in the humanities, it is a recognition that scholars work for a lifetime to obtain. It is often a barometer of a person's contribution to his or her field of specialization. In the past decade or so, this situation has begun to change; however, most professors at Japanese universities and colleges still do not hold a doctoral degree. Thus, even a thorough search of Japanese dissertation catalogs does not guarantee finding a comprehensive bibliography, nor does it necessarily reveal the trend in the field in question.

Although *Nihon hakushiroku* 日本博士録, *Nihon hakushi gakui ronbun sakuin* 日本博士学位論文索引, and *Nihon hakushi gakuiroku* 日本博士学位録 almost correspond to *Dissertation Abstracts International*, there is simply nothing that corresponds to Shulman's works in paper format. However, dissertations are in an online database at the National Diet Library, which is published annually as *Kokuritsu Kokkai Toshokan shozō hakushi ronbun mokuroku* 国立国会図書館所蔵博士論文目録. Publication of this title started with the Shōwa 59–63-nen (1984–88) issue. The library claims to hold 95 percent of the doctoral dissertations written and accepted in Japan. The first volume contains 52,000 dissertations. *Nihon hakushiroku,* although it contains the greatest number of dissertations (approximately 90,000), requires a lot of patience on the part of the user in order to find the needed information because it is arranged by the name of the university that bestowed the degree. The index is divided by the kind of degree. *Nihon hakushi gakui ronbun sakuin* is arranged by subject, while *Nihon hakushi gakuiroku* is arranged by type of doctorate. For Western-language materials, check Shulman's works.

Nihon hakushiroku 1888-March 1962
Nihon hakushi gakui ronbun sakuin March 1958-March 1976
Nihon hakushi gakuiroku March 1976–
Kokuritsu Kokkai Toshokan shozō hakushi ronbun mokuroku 1984–

(Hint for Problem I-7: You are looking for a Japanese dissertation, but there is no particular time frame.)

IMPORTANT GENERAL BIBLIOGRAPHIES DISCUSSED IN THIS CHAPTER

I-1. Pagès, Léon. *Bibliographie japonaise ou catalogue des ouvrages relatifs au Japon qui ont étè publiés depuis le XVe siècle jusqu'à nos jours.* In *Bibliography of the Japanese Empire: 1859–1903.*

I-2. Wenckstern, Friedrich von. *A Bibliography of the Japanese Empire.* Leiden: E. J. Brill, 1895; Tokyo: Maruzen Kabushiki Kaisha, 1907. 2v.

I-3. Nachod, Oskar. *Bibliography of the Japanese Empire 1906–1926.* London: Goldston, 1928. 2v.

I-4. _____. *Bibliographie von Japan 1927–1929, mit Erganzungen für die Jahre 1906-1926.* Leipzig: K. W. Hiersemann, 1931. xiv, 410p.

I-5. _____. *Bibliographie von Japan 1930-1932, mit Erganzungen für die Jahre 1906–1929.* Leipzig: K. W. Hiersemann, 1935. xiv, 351p.

I-6. Praesent, Hans, and Wolf Haenisch. *Bibliographie von Japan 1933–1935, mit Erganzungen für die Jahre 1906–1932.* Leipzig: K. W. Hiersemann, 1937. xi, 452p.

I-7. Haenisch, Wolf, and Hans Praesent. *Bibliographie von Japan 1936–1937, mit Erganzungen für die Jahre 1906–1935.* Leipzig: K. W. Hiersemann, 1940. xi, 569p.

I-8. Pritchard, Earl, ed. *Bulletin of Far Eastern Bibliography.* Washington, D.C.: Committees on Far Eastern Studies of the American Council of Learned Societies, 1936–40. 5v.

I-9. *Cumulative Bibliography of Asian Studies. 1941–1965. 1966–1970. Author Bibliography* and *Subject Bibliography.* Boston: G. K. Hall, 1969–72. 14v.

I-10. *Bibliography of Asian Studies.* Ann Arbor, MI: Association for Asian Studies, 1956–.

I-11. *Index translationum: International Bibliography of Translations.* New Series 1–. Paris: UNESCO, 1948–.

I-12. Shulman, Frank J. *Japan and Korea: An Annotated Bibliography of Doctoral Dissertations in Western Languages, 1877–1969.* Chicago: American Library Association, 1970. 340p.

I-13. _____. *Doctoral Dissertations on Japan and Korea, 1969–1979: An Annotated Bibliography of Studies in Western Languages.* Seattle: University of Washington Press, 1982. xvi, 473p.

I-14. _____. *Doctoral Dissertations on Asia: An Annotated Bibliographical Journal of Current International Research* vol. 1, no. 1 (Winter 1975) and following.

I-15. *An Introductory Bibliography for Japanese Studies.* Tokyo: The Japan Foundation, 1974–.

I-16. *Kokusho sōmokuroku.* Tokyo: Iwanami Shoten, 1963–76. 9v. (Reprint: Tokyo: Iwanami Shoten, 1989–91. 8v. + author index.)

I-17. Kokubungaku Kenkyū Shiryōkan. *Kotenseki sōgō mokuroku.* Tokyo: Iwanami Shoten, 1990. 3v. + index.

I-18. Kokuritsu Kokkai Toshokan, ed. *Kokuritsu Kokkai Toshokan shozō Meijiki kankō tosho mokuroku.* Tokyo: Kokuritsu Kokkai Toshokan, 1971–76. 5v. + index.

I-19. *Teikoku Toshokan Wakan tosho shomei mokuroku.* Tokyo: Teikoku Toshokan, 1899–1944. 10v.

I-20. *Teikoku Toshokan Kokuritsu Toshokan Wakan tosho bunrui mokuroku.* Tokyo: Kokuritsu Kokkai Toshokan, 1964. 1,144p.

I-21. *Kokuritsu Kokkai Toshokan zōsho mokuroku.* 1948–.
    Shōwa 23–33-nen
    Shōwa 34–43-nen
    Shōwa 44–51-nen
    Shōwa 52–60-nen
    Shōwa 61-Heisei 2-nen

I-22. *Zen Nihon shuppanbutsu sōmokuroku.* Shōwa 23-nendo-51-nendo. 1951–78.

I-23. Kokuritsu Kokkai Toshokan, comp. and ed. *Nihon zenkoku shoshi.* Shōwa 52-nenban- (1977–). Tokyo: Kokuritsu Kokkai Toshokan, 1982–.

I-24. *Nihon zenkoku shoshi shūkanban.* 1982–.

Chapter Two
Indexes

Almost every serious nonfiction book has an index. We know by experience how useful good indexes are, and how frustrating it is to use poorly prepared indexes. The indexes we are going to discuss here are not typical content indexes, but they are indexes that identify, or provide access to, periodical and newspaper articles. They are actually bibliographies in a serial form. This type of index tells us about the bibliographic information generally buried within journals, newspapers, or portions of books. When you use periodical indexes, it is important to ask yourself such questions as: Does this index cover the subject adequately? What kind of journals or newspapers does it index? What time period does it cover?

1. PERIODICAL INDEX

Problem II-1. I am looking for an article that appeared in 1988 in *Chanoyu Quarterly*. I know the author of the article is Yanagida Seizan, but I have forgotten the title of the article. Can you help me?

The most well-known, general English-language index to journal articles is the *Reader's Guide to Periodical Literature* (1905–). It first appears in semimonthly installments, which are then incorporated into quarterly publications. A final, cumulative annual volume then covers the period from March through February. The main body of the index contains author and subject entries for journal articles that have appeared in over 200 selected general-interest periodicals published in the United States. In addition, there is a list of author citations for book reviews following the main body of the index. Besides book reviews, it includes ballet, dance, motion picture, musical, opera, records, video, radio and television, and theater reviews.

26   CHAPTER TWO

The *Humanities Index* (v.1, 1974–) is one of two indexes that supersede the *Social Sciences and Humanities Index* (v.19, 1965-v.27, 1974). The main body of the index consists of author and subject entries for periodical articles. Subject fields indexed include archaeology and classical studies, area studies, folklore, history, language and literature, literary and political criticism, performing arts, philosophy, religion and theology, and other related subjects. It appears annually and contains entries for approximately 300 journals. Its companion series, the *Social Sciences Index* (v.1, 1974–), originally published as *International Index* (v.1, 1907-v.18, 1965), is also part of the *Social Sciences and Humanities Index* (v.19, 1965-v.27, 1974). The main body of the *Social Sciences Index* contains author and subject entries for periodical articles in the fields of anthropology, area studies, economics, environmental science, geography, law and criminology, medical sciences, political science, psychology, public administration, sociology, and other related subjects. In addition to the index for approximately 300 journals, it includes book reviews. These indexes contain mainly materials in English, and many other similar indexes in each language exist. For those, consult Eugene Sheehy's *Guide to Reference Books* (V-1) or *Walford's Guide to Reference Materials* (V-2).

(Hint for Problem II-1: You are looking for a journal article that was most likely written in a Western language, probably English.)

Problem II-2.   I want to find the author of the article, "Sengoku makki Satsuma no chanoyu" 戦国末期薩摩の茶の湯, which appeared in *Geinōshi kenkyū* 芸能史研究 in 1987. I also would like to find other articles written by the same author.

Zasshi kiji sakuin: Jinbun shakai hen 雑誌記事索引:人文社会編   (II-1) indexes articles of at least two pages in length that appear in over 1,800 Japanese journals for humanities and social sciences. It excludes essays and literary works. Published quarterly, it is arranged by subject, and each entry includes title, author, title of the journal, volume and number, date and pages, and document identification number. The fourth number of each volume includes a list of all the journal titles indexed, an author index, and a subject index when the subject is a person or corporate body. The five-year cumulative volumes of *Zasshi kiji sakuin,* called *Ruiseki sakuinban* (II-2), can save a lot of time versus looking at individual quarterly volumes.

Sample page of Zasshi kiji sakuin: Jinbun, shakai hen. Ruiseki sakuinban

Indexing journal articles is an important role of the National Diet Library since it is an extremely time-consuming and expensive undertaking for individuals or individual publishers. Caution should be used because the journals indexed in *Zasshi kiji sakuin* are the ones received by the National Diet Library, and sometimes important journals for your field might be missing. This index is especially weak in weekly magazines, both general and subject oriented. For instance, general journals such as *Shūkan Asahi,* and subject journals such as *Shūkan Tōyō keizai, Agora,* and *Gekkan gengo* are missing from this index even though they are important enough to be included. Subject periodical indexes called *xxx[ex. Nihon bungaku] ni kansuru xx[10]-nenkan no zasshi bunken mokuroku,* which are produced by Nichigai Associates, inherit this weakness since their database is constructed on the basis of *Zasshi kiji sakuin.*

For articles that appear in representative general monthly magazines there is *Sōgōshi kiji sakuin 81/87* 総合誌記事索引81/87 (II-3). For articles since July 1987, *Sōgōshi indekkusu* 総合誌インデックス is published semiannually. *Shūkanshi kiji sakuin 81/87* 週刊誌記事索引 81/87 (II-4), an index covering twelve general magazines, is succeeded by the semiannually published *Shūkanshi indekkusu* 週刊誌インデックス.

Ōya Sōichi Bunko zasshi kiji sakuin sōmokuroku 大宅壮一文庫雑誌記事索引総目録 (II-5) is an author and subject index to articles in journals and popular magazines. It was prepared for use in the Ōya Library, the private collection of the famous journalist Ōya Sōichi, but it is also useful as a general index to articles, including those from the Meiji era.

When checking journal articles in your particular field of interest, make sure that the periodical index you are using indexes all the important journals in your field. If any of the important ones are missing, you will need to supplement the information with other sources. Besides many other periodical indexes similar to the prototype *Zasshi kiji sakuin,* major journals and yearbooks in many fields index journal articles. *Kokubungaku nenkan* 国文学年鑑, *Kokugo nenkan* 国語年鑑, and *Nihon bijutsu nenkan* 日本美術年鑑 are only a few. When you need to search journal articles written prior to 1948, the year *Zasshi kiji sakuin* started, you have to use appropriate bibliographies and indexes in your special subject area. For those, consult *Nihon no sankō tosho: Kaisetsu sōran* (V-3). Also familiarize yourself with some core journals, major current bibliographies, periodical indexes, and abstracts, if any, in your field, and check them on a regular basis to supplement your information file and to fill the time lag in the publication of indexes. Many articles in Japanese academic publications are not, in fact, definitive versions of a scholar's opinions, a rather different situation from that in the West.

(Hint for Problem II-2: Begin with a subject search.)

Quiz II-1. I need to find the journal in which Gomi Katsuo wrote an article titled "Kamakura Bakufu no banshū to kubunin" 鎌倉幕府の番衆と供奉人.

2. NEWSPAPER INDEX

Problem II-3. How were the deaths of Mishima Yukio 三島由紀夫 and Kawabata Yasunari 川端康成 perceived in the United States? Were the responses to their deaths different in any way?

A newspaper index is very useful when you are looking for a particular incident as long as you have a fairly good idea when that event happened. A good example of a newspaper index is the *New York Times Index: A Book of Record*. It starts in September 1851 and continues to the present. It first appears in semimonthly installments, which are incorporated into quarterly indexes; these are then combined into a permanent, annual cumulative volume. Short news is included in each entry, along with many *see also* references. This index is one of the best because of the wide scope of its coverage and completeness.

If the news is internationally noteworthy or likely to have been reported by the *New York Times* or the *Wall Street Journal*, it is faster to go to the indexes of those publications than to look through Japanese newspapers, which do not have a cumulative index.

If the news is not internationally noteworthy, unless you can afford to use on-line database services such as Nikkei TELECOM NEWS/RETRIEVAL or CD-HIASK, you will have to search for information in Japanese newspapers. You can easily obtain information if you know the date of the event. If you know the month and year but not the day, you can use the index at the end of the reduced-size edition (*shukusatsuban* 縮刷版) of the paper of your choice. Major newspapers publish a reduced-size edition with an index. *Asahi Shinbun kiji sōran* 朝日新聞記事総覧 (II-6) is an index to *Asahi Shinbun shukusatsuban* 朝日新聞縮刷版. Its coverage begins in the Taishō era. If the year of the event is known but not the month, you may also use indexes of *Yomiuri nyūsu sōran: Nyūsu kiji no sakuin to shōroku* 読売ニュース総覧 (II-7) or *nenkan*, such as *Asahi nenkan* 朝日年鑑, *Mainichi nenkan* 毎日年鑑, *Yomiuri nenkan* 読売年鑑, and *Jiji nenkan* 時事年鑑. Each newspaper's indexing categories are different, and you might have to search under different terms from paper to paper. CD-HIASK is the CD-ROM version of the Asahi Shinbun Kiji Database. Except for the sports, culture, and family and home columns, the year's information from the morning and evening papers are on this CD.

Meiji nyūsu jiten 明治ニュース事典 (II-8), *Taishō nyūsu jiten* 大正ニュース事典 (II-9), and *Shōwa nyūsu jiten* 昭和ニュース事典 (II-10) are convenient and equipped with various indexes to find news information. If a library does not have these titles, *Shinbun shūsei Meiji hennenshi* 新聞集成明治編年史 (II-11) (v. 15 is the index), *Shinbun shūsei Taishō hennenshi* 新聞集成大正編年史 (II-12), and *Shinbun shūsei Shōwa hennenshi* 新聞集成昭和編年史 (II-13) also can be used for retrospective searches.

(Hint for Problem II-3: How about checking the *New York Times*?)

Quiz II-2. Natsume Sōseki declined the doctoral degree. Was it from the Imperial University of Tokyo or from the Ministry of Education? When did this happen, and why? (Hint: When was he born, or when did he die?)

IMPORTANT PERIODICAL INDEXES DISCUSSED IN THIS CHAPTER

II-1. Kokuritsu Kokkai Toshokan, comp. *Zasshi kiji sakuin: Jinbun shakai hen.* Tokyo: Kokuritsu Kokkai Toshokan, 1948–.

II-2. *Zasshi kiji sakuin: Jinbun shakai hen. Ruiseki sakuinban.* Tokyo: Kokuritsu Kokkai Toshokan, 1948–.

II-3. *Sōgōshi kiji sakuin 81/87.* Tokyo: Nichigai Asoshieitsu, 1988. 3v.

II-4. *Shūkanshi kiji sakuin 81/87.* Tokyo: Nichigai Asoshieitsu, 1988. 3v.

II-5. *Ōya Sōichi Bunko zasshi kiji sakuin sōmokuroku.* Tokyo: Ōya Sōichi Bunko, 1985–88. 17v.

II-6. *Asahi Shinbun kiji sōran.* Tokyo: Nihon Tosho Sentaa, 1985–.

II-7. *Yomiuri nyūsu sōran: Nyūsu kiji no sakuin to shōroku.* Tokyo: Yomiuri Shinbunsha, 1978–.

II-8. *Meiji nyūsu jiten.* Tokyo: Mainichi Komyunikeishonzu, 1983–86. 9v.

II-9. *Taishō nyūsu jiten.* Tokyo: Mainichi Komyunikeishonzu, 1986–89. 8v.

II-10. *Shōwa nyūsu jiten.* Tokyo: Mainichi Komyunikeishonzu, 1990–.

II-11. Nakayama Yasumasa, ed. *Shinbun shūsei Meiji hennenshi.* Tokyo: Meiji Hennenshi Hensankai, 1934–36. 15v.

II-12. *Shinbun shūsei Taishō hennenshi.* Tokyo: Taishō Shōwa Shinbun Kenkyūkai. 1966–.

II-13. *Shinbun shūsei Shōwa hennenshi.* Tokyo: Shinbun Shūsei Taishō Shōwa Hennenshi Kankōkai, 1955–.

Chapter Three
Publishers' Catalogs

What purpose does a publisher's catalog serve in a bibliographic search when you are writing a thesis? It can be used to verify bibliographic information, and it can tell you what is available in case you want to purchase books.

1. BOOKS

Books in Print (1948–) is widely used and well known. It covers every type of book published in the United States and available for purchase at the time of its compilation. It is useful for finding the publisher, price, author's name (if only the title is known), or title (if only the author's name is known), and for searching by subject. Each entry includes the author, coauthor, editor, price, publisher, date of publication (usually), number of volumes, LC card number (mainly for library use), and ISBN.[1] Directories of publishers are also included. It is produced annually from the database with the same name (BIPS) by the R. R. Bowker Company and lists all in-print and forthcoming titles from approximately 50,000 publishers. It includes both trade books and textbooks and has sections for titles and authors and a subject guide (excluding fiction, poetry, and the Bible). A supplement is published between appearances of the annual. There are separate volumes for paperback books, *Paperbound Books in Print*. The *Cumulative Book Index* (CBI) is by far the most comprehen-

---

1. International Standard Book Number. Every edition of every title should have its own, unique ISBN number to aid in identification, to avoid possible mix-ups with books of the same title, and to speed up the ordering process.

sive catalog of books printed in the English language. CBI is an international author, title, and subject index for both current books and those in publication since 1898. Government publications, most pamphlets, inexpensive paperbound books, and nonbook formats are excluded. All index entries are in a single alphabetical listing. The user can search by author, subject, and title, but the full bibliographic information is given under the main entry. CBI should be used when you are looking for bibliographic data for a book whose publication date you know.

Problem III-1. I would like to purchase *Zuroku chadōshi* 図録茶道史 by Hayashiya Tatsusaburō 林屋辰三郎, which was published in 1980. Who was the publisher and how much did it cost? Is it still available?

Shuppan nenkan 出版年鑑 (III-1) lists books and periodicals published during the previous year. This can be used as a supplement to *Nihon zenkoku shoshi* (I-23) when the publication date is known. The 1992 edition includes over 42,000 items classified by Nippon Decimal Classification,[2] which is fairly similar to Dewey Decimal Classification. It contains most trade books, but important government publications and other nontrade research materials are not covered fully. It also contains such features as an overview of publishing and related industries, awards, statistics, and directories of publishers. It has indexes for titles and authors, translators, or compilers, and also current journal titles. *Shuppan nenkan* is the annual cumulative volume of *Shuppan nyūsu* 出版ニュース, which is published three times a month and has current information about new publications along with news items and articles related to publishing.

Nihon shoseki sōmokuroku 日本書籍総目録 (III-2) is the Japanese version of *Books in Print*. The 1993 edition includes 463,226 items published by 5,850 publishers. This is an annual publication and covers over 90 percent of the total number of publications currently available. Information includes books that have been published by

---

2. Nippon Decimal Classification is basically the Dewey Decimal Classification System with some elaboration of the Japanese and Asian culture sections. Public libraries and small- to medium-sized academic libraries in Japan use this system.

CHAPTER THREE

第2巻								歴史総記
2 歴 史								
著訳編者	書 名		判型	頁	定価	発行所・発行月	NDC	
20 歴史総記	0 歴史総記 1 歴史学 2 歴史の補助学 3 書誌.辞典.便覧.年表.歴史			図など 4 論文・講演集. 歴史評論.史話. 雑著 5 逐次刊行物.年鑑		6 学会.団体.会議 7 研究・指導法. 歴史教育 8 叢書.全集.合集 9 世界史.文化史		
樺山 紘一 編	中公新書 926 現代歴史学の名著		B40	221	580	中央公論社⑥	201	
ハーヴェイ J. ・ケイ 桜井 清 監訳	イギリスのマルクス主義歴史家たち		A5	367	3500	白桃書房⑦	〃	
ドミニク・ラカプラ 前川 裕 訳	テオリア叢書 歴 史 と 批 評		A5	221	2890	平 凡 社⑧	〃	
竹本 秀彦	エルンスト・トレルチと歴史的世界		B6	318	2800	行 路 社⑩	201.1	
アーサー・C・ダント	物語としての歴史		A5	390	4200	国 文 社②	〃	
R・コゼレック	フィロソフィア双書 25 批 判 と 危 機		B6	340	3500	未 来 社③	〃	
オスヴァルト・シュペングラー	西 洋 の 没 落 第1巻		A5	393	3914	五 月 書 房⑤	〃	
オスヴァルト・シュペングラー	西 洋 の 没 落 第2巻		A5	414	3914	五 月 書 房⑤	〃	
C.・セニョボス C.V.・ラングロア	歴史学研究入門		B6	272	3090	校倉書房⑤	201.16	
国際歴史学会議編	日本における歴史学の発達と現状 7（1983-1987）		A5	358	3800	山川出版社⑫	201.2	
日本歴史地理学会編集	歴 史 地 理 35～48巻		A5	14冊	210000	第 一 書 房②	202.2	
慶応義塾大学 編	考 古 学 の 世 界		A5	638	9800	新人物往来社⑥	202.5	
竹岡 俊樹	石 器 研 究 法		A5	366	5600	言 叢 社②	〃	
樋岡 謙二郎 編集代表	講座 考古地理学 5		A5	213	3450	学 生 社⑨	〃	
渡辺仁教授古稀記念論文集刊行会編	考古学と民族誌		B5	346	9200	六 興 出 版⑫	〃	
ヘルムート・トリノッチ 渡 辺 正 訳	歴 気 楼 文 明		A5	302	2900	工 作 舎⑪	〃	
川比野 丈夫 編	世 界 史 年 表		B6	633	1800	河出書房新社⑫	203.2	
平 田 俊春	最 新 歴 史 年 表		A5	337	2900	朋 友 出 版⑦	〃	
赤 坂 憲雄	ディヴィニタス叢書 1 境 界 の 発 生		B6	370	2500	砂子屋書房④	204	
阿 部 謹也	社 会 史 と は 何 か		A5	308	2160	筑 摩 書 房⑨	〃	

Sample page of Shuppan nenkan

the end of previous year and are available as of May of the current year. Journals, government publications, nationally approved textbooks, books not for sale, and sheet maps are not included. There are indexes arranged by author and series, and an appendix with a directory of publishers and publishing statistics. Unlike *Books in Print,* there is no subject guide, which is a serious weakness.

To bridge the gap in materials not covered by *Nihon shoseki sōmokuroku,* you need to check catalogs of government publications and other specific catalogs as well as *Nihon zenkoku shoshi.*

(Hint for Problem III-1: You cannot always tell whether a work is available solely by consulting *Shuppan nenkan*.)

There are numerous bookstores of various sizes in Japan, and they sell mostly new books and magazines. There are also many secondhand book dealers of both high-quality and cheap books. The Kanda (Jinbōchō) area in Tokyo is especially famous for its concentration of hundreds of secondhand bookstores. Many other used bookstores are scattered all over Japan, particularly in areas around large universities, such as the Hongo area near the University of Tokyo, which is the second largest concentration of such bookstores in Tokyo. Some stores specialize in particular subjects, and many of them publish their own sales catalogs. Information on or guides to bookstores or book-selling areas of large Japanese cities are available from major Japanese collections in the United States.

Quiz III-1. I would like to purchase the book, *Nihon kodai bunkaken no keisei to denpa*, published in 1991, I believe. Who is the publisher and how much does it cost? Is it still available?

Quiz III-2. I heard that Tōkyō Daigaku Shakai Kagaku Kenkyūjo is compiling a series called *Gendai Nihon shakai* 現代日本社会, or something close to that. I would like to get more information about it.

(Hint: Information on a recent publication is most difficult to obtain. If the information you need is about a recently published book, a search through *Shuppan nyūsu* should be helpful, although tedious.)

Problem III-2. Was *Chadō shūkin* 茶道集錦, a monographic series published by Shōgakkan, completed?

Zenshū sōgō mokuroku 全集総合目録, a companion title of *Shuppan nenkan*, lists the contents of collected works and monographic series but does not include children's books, study aids, maps, or journals. It includes title indexes in Japanese syllabary order.

(Hint for Problem III-2: If necessary, combine information obtained from *Zenshū sōgō mokuroku*, *Nihon zenkoku shoshi*, *Shuppan nenkan*, or *Nihon shoseki sōmokuroku*.)

36   CHAPTER THREE

Quiz III-3. Has the last volume been published of *Taikei Nihon shi sōsho* 体系日本史叢書, a monographic series published by Yamakawa Shuppansha? If so, is it obtainable?

2. PERIODICALS

Ulrich's International Periodicals Directory is a classified guide to current periodicals, foreign and domestic. The 1992–93 edition has entries for approximately 126,000 selected, current periodicals published throughout the world by over 67,000 publishers in about 200 countries are arranged alphabetically by title into 788 subject headings. This directory includes periodicals that are currently available. When checking what is available in a particular field, turn first to the subject guide, then to the classified list of periodicals that constitutes the main body of the directory. Each entry lists the periodicals that index the articles carried in that journal. *Ulrich's* is also available online, in CD-ROM format, and on microfiche.

Problem III-3. I want to find the publisher and address of a journal called *Chadō no kenkyū* 茶道の研究.

Nihon zasshi sōran 日本雑誌総覧 (III-3) corresponds to *Ulrich's,* except that its scope is limited to serials published in Japan. It began publication in 1963 and has been frequently revised. The 1988 edition lists approximately 23,000 titles of currently published serials. This can be used when you want to subscribe to a journal or to verify information.

Nihon shinbun zasshi benran 日本新聞雑誌便覧 (III-4) is an annual classified directory of publishers of newspapers and journals in Japanese syllabary order. It can be used to supplement *Nihon zasshi sōran.* It contains the name and address of the publisher, the characteristics of the company, and the founding date, title, circulation, and price of the newspaper or journal. It is arranged by subject. An index to company names is included. *Zasshi shinbun sōkatarogu* 雑誌新聞総かたろぐ (III-5) is a convenient and useful annual publication that tries to include all serial publications arranged into 274 genres. The 1992 edition includes 15,474 serials and 3,665 newspapers totaling 19,139 titles from 10,500 publishers.

It has been very difficult until recently to acquire information on annual publications. Now, with the expansion of *Kokuritsu Kokkai Toshokan shozō kokunai chikuji kankōbutsu mokuroku* (IV-5) to include annuals and with the publication of *Nenkan hakusho zenjōhō 45/89* 年鑑白書全情報 (III-6) and *Nihon nenkan sōran* 日本年鑑総覧 (III-7), this task has become much easier.

(Hint for Problem III-3: The list of journals in *Shuppan nenkan* could also provide the latest information.)

Quiz III-4. I want to find out the publisher and address of a journal called *Hikaku bungaku kenkyū*. The first number was published in 1954.

(Hint: Sometimes, different journals with the same title may be published by separate agencies or groups. Be aware of the date in this case.)

Quiz III-5. What newspapers in the United States are published in Japanese?

(Hint: Other types of reference tools are also often helpful, such as *Shinbun nenkan*.)

IMPORTANT PUBLISHERS' CATALOGS DISCUSSED IN THIS CHAPTER

III-1. *Shuppan nenkan*. Tokyo: Shuppan Nyūsusha, 1950–. An annual cumulative volume of *Shuppan nyūsu* (Tokyo: Shuppan Nyūsusha). For predecessors of this catalog back to the Meiji era, refer to *Nihon no sankō tosho: Kaisetsu sōran* (V-3).

III-2. *Nihon shoseki sōmokuroku*. Tokyo: Nihon Shoseki Shuppan Kyōkai, 1977/78–.

III-3. *Nihon zasshi sōran*. Tokyo: Shuppan Nyūsusha, 1963–.

III-4. *Nihon shinbun zasshi benran*. Tokyo: Nihon Shinbun Zasshi Chōsakai Masukomi Shiryō Sentaa, 1962–.

III-5. *Zasshi shinbun sōkatarogu*. Tokyo: Media Risachi Sentaa, 1979–.

III-6. *Nenkan hakusho zenjōhō 45/89*. Tokyo: Nichigai Asoshieitsu, 1991. 11, 963p.

III-7. Shoshi Kenkyūkai, comp. *Nihon nenkan sōran*. Tokyo: Nihon Tosho Sentaa, 1987.

Chapter Four
Library Catalogs

Whether it is in on-line or card format, the library catalog indicates the location of books and serials and lists all the books the library owns. In most libraries the catalog lists books by author or editor, title, and subject matter.

Although knowledge of how to use a card catalog is essential in conducting library research, searching library catalogs, particularly card catalogs, is not as simple as it might seem. You may need to know some basic filing rules to conduct efficient library research. Though many libraries in the United States and Canada use ALA (American Library Association) filing rules, some East Asian libraries might have different rules, particularly for the author and title catalog of vernacular materials. When you have problems, do not hesitate to ask your librarian for help. It might save you a great deal of time and effort because for many students library research is often confusing and frustrating.[1]

Many libraries are switching to on-line catalogs, but at the same time, many of them still maintain a separate card catalog, sometimes in book catalog format. It is very important to be aware of the peculiarity of the library you are using. Here we will concentrate on book catalogs as location lists. Books in the library you are using can be found through the card catalog, but what about the books not owned by your library? Often, they can be obtained from another library through the interlibrary loan service.

1. BOOKS

Problem IV-1. Which library in the United States owns *Nihon chadōshi* 日本茶道史 by Kuwata Tadachika 桑田忠親?

1. For basic filing rules, see chapter eleven.

40　CHAPTER FOUR

The *National Union Catalog* (NUC) (IV-1) of the Library of Congress is a universal bibliography that actually comprises three different catalogs. The first is the *National Union Catalog: Author List* (1956–); the second is the *National Union Catalog: Pre-1956 Imprints* (IV-2, 685 volumes); and the third is the *Library of Congress Catalogs: Subject Catalog* (1950–). NUC is basically made up of reproductions of Library of Congress main entry cards (commonly called LC cards) and titles reported by other North American libraries, with location symbols added following the bibliographic information.

Hachidaishū.
　　(Hachidaishū)
　　八代集 ／ 奥村恒哉校注. ― 初版. ― 東京：平凡社, 1986–
　　　　v. ; 18 cm. ―（東洋文庫 ; 452–　）
　　Includes bibliographies.
　　Contents: 1. Kokin wakashū. Gosen wakashū
　　ISBN 4582804527 (v. 1)

　　1. Waka.　　2. Japanese poetry—1600.　　I. Okumura, Tsuneya,
1927–　　II. Series: Tōyō bunko ; 452, etc.
PL758.2.H3　1986　　　　　　　　　　　　　　　86-138989
　　　　　　　　　　　　　　　　　　　　　　　　　　MARC
　　　　　　　　　　　　　　　　　　　　　　　　　AACR 2
　　Library of Congress　　　　86　　　　　　　　　　AJ

Library of Congress Card (LC Card)

For current materials that do not appear in printed catalogs, on-line catalog databases such as RLIN-CJK[2] and OCLC-CJK,[3] to which the Library of Congress supplies cataloging information on Japanese, Chinese, and Korean language materials, are a handy way of checking which institution owns the books or journals you want to borrow or of verifying the bibliographic information. Both of these databases have bibliographic information in Japanese, which reduces much vagueness or ambiguity. Both databases contain growing num-

---

2. Research Libraries Information Network-Chinese, Japanese, Korean.
3. On-line Computer Library Center-Chinese, Japanese, Korean.

bers of Japanese materials. Ask your librarian if your library participates in these programs.

The NUC of the Library of Congress is not a very effective tool for locating Japanese books in North America. Instead, printed catalogs of individual libraries with East Asian collections, such as those of the University of California at Berkeley (*East Asiatic Library. University of California, Berkeley. Author-Title Catalog*), the University of Chicago (*Catalogs of the Far Eastern Library. University of Chicago*), the Harvard-Yenching Library (*Chinese and Japanese Catalogues of the Harvard-Yenching Library*), the Hoover Institution (*The Library Catalogs of the Hoover Institution on War, Revolution, and Peace. Stanford University: Catalog of the Japanese Collection*), and the University of Michigan (*Catalogs of the Asia Library. The University of Michigan, Ann Arbor*) together function as the NUC for Japanese-language materials in the United States.

(Hint for Problem IV-1: Without knowing the date of publication, you will need some perseverance in searching. You first might want to check the date of publication by using the title index of *Nihon choshamei sōmokuroku*, which covers books published between 1945 and 1988.)

Quiz IV-1. Which library in the United States owns *Teihon Kinoshita Yūji shishū* 定本木下夕爾詩集?

Problem IV-2. No libraries in the United States own *Echigo Mōrishi no kenkyū* 越後毛利氏の研究 written by Seki Hisashi 関久 and published by Jōetsu Kyōdo Kenkyūkai 上越郷土研究会 in 1965. Is there any Japanese library that owns this book?

The Japanese counterpart of the NUC at the Gakujutsu Jōhō Sentaa (National Center for Science Information System [NACSIS]) is still too small to be useful for searches. There are some tools for general use, however. Those are *Kokusho sōmokuroku* (I-16) and *Kotenseki sōgō mokuroku* (I-17) for pre-Meiji materials, and catalogs I-19 through I-24 of the National Diet Library, which are mentioned under section 2 of chapter one. Most libraries registered in *Kokusho sōmokuroku* and the NDL provide copying services or international interlibrary loan services. Information on the holdings of other libraries can

42   CHAPTER FOUR

only be obtained from their published catalogs, if any, or through direct correspondence with them.

(Hint for Problem IV-2: If no location is identified in the catalogs mentioned, direct correspondence with the author or the publisher will be the most effective next step.)

2. SERIALS

Problem IV-3. What libraries in the United States own *Monumenta Nipponica*?

    The *Union List of Serials in Libraries of the United States and Canada* (IV-3), which covers the years up to 1949, and its continuation, *New Serial Titles* (1950–) (IV-4), are union lists of many libraries in North America, and include the titles of numerous serials published in all countries. They also contain cross-references to deal with title changes. In 1981 *New Serial Titles* became a product of CONSER (Cooperative On-line Serials) Program,[4] and coverage was expanded to include reports of all serials contributed to the CONSER file, regardless of the date of publication. The information is presented in a catalog-card format and the completeness of the record depend on the amount of data reported.

    For journals in Western languages, Nunn's *Japanese Periodicals and Newspapers in Western Languages: An International Union List* can be used to supplement *New Serial Titles* and the *Union List of Serials*. Nunn's list, which covers the period from the 1860s to 1978, is the first comprehensive list of international holdings of Japanese periodicals and newspapers written in Western languages in all fields. The information is collected from sources such as the *Union List of Serials, New Serial Titles,* and the *British Union-Catalogue of Periodicals*. Most of the holding libraries are located in Great Britain, the United States, Japan, and Canada. The serials are listed alphabetically by title, and variant titles are included.

    For Japanese journals currently received in the United States and Canada, it is more convenient to use the *National Union List of*

---

4. CONSER was previously known as Conversion of Serials.

LIBRARY CATALOGS   43

Japanese Serials in Current East Asian Libraries of North America (IV-5). This list covers Japanese language serials currently received by East Asian collections, and it includes 5,000 journals not only in the humanities and social sciences, but also in science and other subject areas. For journals not found in this list, check on-line for holdings in the Library of Congress and the Center for Research Libraries.

For journal articles that appeared in Japanese serials and cannot be obtained in North America, you might have to extend your search to Japan. But before that, contact the Library of Congress for information. You can also access the NACSIS database through INTERNET, and that procedure may be helpful. For details, consult your librarian.

Kokuritsu Kokkai Toshokan shozō kokunai chikuji kankōbutsu mokuroku 国立国会図書館所蔵国内逐次刊行物目録 (1987–) (IV-6) is the new title for *Kokuritsu Kokkai Toshokan shozō wazasshi mokuroku* 国立国会図書館所蔵和雑誌目録. As you can see from the new title, the publisher has widened its scope to include newspapers, annuals, and yearbooks as well as Western-language serials published in Japan. The first issue includes close to 60,000 titles.

Gakujutsu zasshi sōgō mokuroku: Wabun hen 学術雑誌総合目録：和文編 (1992, 7v.) (IV-7), the national union list of Japanese scholarly (in the broad sense of the word) journals, including annuals, is the product of an on-line database of the same name based at the Gakujutsu Jōhō Sentaa. This latest published edition includes the serial holdings of over 600 academic and governmental libraries, and contains close to 40,000 titles and approximately a million entries. This number is constantly increasing as more and more libraries are connecting to this system. Cross-references are made for all variant titles. The index is arranged in Japanese syllabary order for Japanese titles and in alphabetical order for foreign or romanized titles. Revision of the published edition is in progress.

(Hint for Problem IV-3: No particular issue is requested.)

Quiz IV-2: Does the University of Illinois own the 1977 issues of *Kokka gakkai zasshi* 国家学会雑誌？

Let's review the process for a bibliographic search step by step. First, collect the bibliographic information necessary for your

社會思想　(*00407286*)
　　社會思想社　1巻1號(1922.4)-9巻1号
　　(1930.1)
　　東京　社会思想社
北大〔2〕, 4, 〔5-7〕　北海大〔4〕, 〔6〕, 〔8〕
東北大〔5-6〕　東院大〔3-5〕, 〔7〕, 8, 〔9〕
東大　1, 〔2〕, 3-8, 〔9〕　東大法史〔1-7〕　一橋
　　〔3〕, 4-5, 〔6〕　一橋経研〔9〕　都大　7-8
　　慶大三　1-2, 〔3-4〕, 5-8　国学院　1-8　ICU
　　〔7〕　中大〔5〕, 6, 〔7-8〕　日大経〔3〕　法大　1-
　　3, 〔4-5〕, 〔7-8〕　法大大　1-9
名市大経　1-7
京大法　6-7　京大経　3-7, 〔8〕　京大人〔1-3〕, 4-
　　6, 〔7-9〕　和大　4-8, 〔9〕　阪市大　1, 〔4〕, 〔6-
　　7〕, 8　同大　1-8　立命館〔1-8〕　天理大〔1-
　　6〕
山口大〔2〕, 8　香大〔1〕
九大　6-9　佐大〔1-7〕　西南院〔2〕

Sample page of Gakujutsu zasshi sōgō mokuroku

research by using the bibliographies, periodical indexes, and abstracts in chapters one and two. Do you have all the bibliographic information you need? Do you know the author, title (both the title of the article and the title of the journal in the case of journal articles), publisher, and place and date of publication? If you are missing any of the above information, turn for help to *Nihon zenkoku shoshi, Gakujutsu zasshi sōgō mokuroku: Wabun hen,* or other bibliographies, indexes, and catalogs.

　　Second, find out where these books and journals are located. To make a thorough search within the United States, use NUC, NST, and the printed catalogs of large East Asian collections. For more recent publications, particularly those appearing after 1983, search on-line in databases such as RLIN-CJK or OCLC-CJK.

Third, acquire the material through interlibrary loan at your local university library if it does not have the books or journals you need. Note that interlibrary loan will normally take a few weeks to a month, depending on where the volume is held. For journal articles in Japanese, we have a union list of Japanese serials that covers all of North America. If no holding library is found within North America, you will have to search for a location in Japan. Since there is nothing that corresponds to NUC in Japan, start with the book catalogs of the National Diet Library or the book catalogs of special collections. For journals check first the serial catalog of National Diet Library or *Gakujutsu zasshi sōgō mokuroku: Wabun hen*. The National Diet Library actively participates in the international interlibrary loan service. Your librarian will help you to acquire the journal article or book you need. If you want to purchase books published in Japan, there are book dealers who specialize in exporting books overseas, such as the Japan Publications Trading Company. Ask your librarian for their addresses.

IMPORTANT PERIODICAL LISTS DISCUSSED IN THIS CHAPTER

IV-1. *National Union Catalog: A Cumulative Author List Representing Library of Congress Printed Cards and Titles Reported by Other American Libraries.* Washington, D.C.: Library of Congress, 1956–. This catalog has been published in microform since 1983.

IV-2. *National Union Catalog, Pre-1956 Imprints. A Cumulative Author List Representing Library of Congress Printed Cards and Titles Reported by Other American Libraries.* London: Mansell, 1968–80. 685v.

IV-3. Titus, Edna Brown. *Union List of Serials in Libraries of the United States and Canada*, 3d ed. New York: H.W. Wilson, 1965. 5v.

IV-4. *New Serial Titles: A Union List of Serials Commencing Publication after December 31, 1949.* Washington, D.C.: Library of Congress, 1953–. In 1981, this became a product of CONSER.

IV-5. Makino, Yasuko and Mihoko Miki, with the assistance of Isamu Miura and Kenji Niki, comps. and eds. *National Union List of Japanese Serials in Current East Asian Libraries of North America.* Los Angeles, CA: Subcommittee on Japanese Materials, Committee on East Asian Libraries, Association for Asian Studies, 1992. 485p.

IV-6. *Kokuritsu Kokkai Toshokan shozō kokunai chikuji kankōbutsu mokuroku.* Tokyo: Kokuritsu Kokkai Toshokan, 1987–.

IV-7. *Gakujutsu zasshi sōgō mokuroku: Wabun hen.* Tokyo: Monbushō Gakujutsu Kokusaikyoku. 1985–.

Chapter Five
Guides to Reference Tools

A guide to reference books gives the major sources of information for a particular subject area and also explains how to find and use the information contained in the sources. The main purpose of this book is to familiarize students in the field of Japanese studies with the most important reference works. We intentionally have not included too many reference books so that the basic ones will attract your attention. Sooner or later, you will need to use more specialized reference books; for now, however, you must learn to use guides to standard Japanese reference works, or more specifically, guides to reference works related to Japanese studies, which annotate bibliographies and other reference works of various types.

Problem V-1. Is there any bibliography on the tea ceremony?

Problem V-2. Where can I find the statistics for people who committed suicide using city gas? I need to have the figures for five years prior to Kawabata's death.

A general and basic guide to reference works such as bibliographies, handbooks, and dictionaries is Sheehy's *Guide to Reference Books* (V-1), which tells you what important reference books are available in all major fields. It is international in scope, although it concentrates on American, Canadian, and English titles. It lists and annotates the major titles used in reference services at libraries. Complete bibliographical information is given for each entry. It begins with broad subject categories and then subdivides them into narrower subjects and forms. A supplement by Richard Balay (V-2) brings coverage up through 1990. The book is updated by journal articles written by the compiler in the January issue of *College and*

Research Libraries. *Walford's Guide to Reference Materials* (V-3) is the British version of Sheehy's *Guide*. This is also international in scope, but with an emphasis on items published in Great Britain.

The updated and much-enlarged edition of *Nihon no sankō tosho: Kaisetsu sōran* 日本の参考図書：解説総覧 (V-4) guides its users to appropriate reference works published in Japan from 1868 through 1977. About 5,500 titles are annotated, and an additional 770 are mentioned in other related annotations. It covers all fields and is arranged by category: general, humanities, social sciences, natural science, and technology. Each of these sections is further divided into more specific subject areas. The guide includes both a title and a subject index, and it is updated by *Saikin no sankō tosho 1981–82* (a continuation of *Gendai no toshokan*) and quarterly supplements called *Nihon no sankō tosho: Shikiban* 日本の参考図書：四季版. Cumulative supplements have been published every few years.

Nihon no sankō tosho is more useful for Japanese studies than general guides such as Sheehy's, but the following are specifically designed for students and researchers in Japanese studies and annotate reference works particularly pertaining to Japanese studies. The *Bibliography of Reference Works for Japanese Studies* 日本の参考図書 - 人文 社会編 (V-5), by Naomi Fukuda, one of the original compilers of *Nihon no sankō tosho,* also includes some reference works on Japan written in English. Two subject areas, education and law, are not covered in this guide. Its arrangement is similar to *Nihon no sankō tosho* but differs in its inclusion of source materials and large collections, which are not normally considered reference works. *A Guide to Reference Books for Japanese Studies* 日本研究のための参考図書 (V-6), a more current work designed for supplementary use with the former, also includes large numbers of English-language materials. These two works are convenient for those who are not fluent in reading Japanese because both of them provide selected Japanese reference works with concise English annotations.

The above-mentioned guides are the various reference tools that you will need for Japanese studies in general. It is also very useful to know *Shoshi nenkan* 書誌年鑑, a guide to bibliographies and catalogs. By checking the information sources included in this yearbook of bibliography, you can conduct a comprehensive, current bibliographic search.

| エイヨ | 事項索引 |

栄養士　ⒹEC140, ⒽEC153, 159	エンジン　→内燃機関
⇌給食	演奏家　→音楽家
英和辞典　→英語—辞書(英和)	
駅　ⓃCF35	
疫学　→予防医学	
液化石油ガス　→LPガス	**【オ】**
エコロジー　→生態．生態学	
SF　ⒷBH24	
エスペラント　ⒷBG381, ⒹBG	欧州　→ヨーロッパ
382—384, ⒽBG385	王朝文学　→日本文学—歴史—平
エチオピア語　ⒹBG205—207	時代
江戸　ⒸBC198	欧米　→アメリカ合衆国．ヨーロ
⇌東京．日本—歴史—江戸時代	パ
江戸—史跡　BD9	オウム　ⓅEA107
江戸—地誌　BD10—14	応用植物　→有用植物
江戸—風俗　ⒹCH30—39	応用動物　→有用動物
江戸絵　→浮世絵	応用物理学　→工業物理学
江戸時代　→日本—歴史—江戸時代	往来物　→教科書
江戸文学　→日本文学—歴史—江戸	OR　→オペレーションズ・リサ

CH31

江戸生活事典　三田村鳶魚　稲垣史生編　青蛙房

昭和34(1959)　541p

『武家事典』(CH38)の続編であるが，三田村氏の著作からでは資料不足または欠けているものは他の著者から補足してある。旅と飛脚・財政経済の実際・火消の制度・僧と庶民・やくざと非人・女人・風俗一般等江戸の生活事象の主要なものを網羅してある。付録に出典一覧表・江戸時代通貨表・江戸風俗年表・江戸生活時刻表，巻末に事項索引がある。

Sample Page from Nihon no sankō tosho: Kaisetsu sōran

367　婦人・家庭・性問題

'84. 10　p 2 — 10　　　　　　　　　　　　　　　　　　　　　　[0557]

367　婦人・家庭・性問題

○参考文献　「婦人解放と結婚の将来」(嶋田津矢子著)　(京都)ミネルヴァ書房 (関西学院大学研究叢書49)　'85. 3　p 252—257　　　　　　　　　　[0558]
◎「東京都婦人情報センター所蔵資料目録　婦人関係新聞・雑誌編」同センター編刊　'85. 3　97p B 5　　　　　　　　　　　　　　　　　　　　　[0559]
◎「女性問題図書総目録　1985」東販内同総目録刊行会編刊　'85. 4　165p A 5　300円　(注)解説付　(付)書名索引　著者索引　シリーズ索引　　　[0560]
◎参考文献　「女を装う」(町野美和ほか著　駒尺喜美編)　勁草書房　'85. 6　p 216—218　　　　　　　　　　　　　　　　　　　　　　　　　　　[0561]
○戦後の日本女性史研究をめぐって(友野清文)　「東京大学教育学部教育史・教育哲学研究室」11　'85. 6　p 116—123　　　　　　　　　　　　　[0562]
◎新・女性と法関係文献(橋本ヒロ子，馬場浩子)　「女性そして男性」日本評論社(法学セミナー増刊総合特集シリーズ30)　'85. 6　p 268—275　[0563]
◎参考文献　「女性の自立とライフ・サイクル」(森主一，村尾勇之編著)　家政教育社　'85. 8　p 174—176　　　　　　　　　　　　　　　　　　[0564]
○「国連婦人の十年」年表掲載資料リスト(国立婦人教育会館情報交流課)　「婦人教育情報」(埼玉県嵐山町　国立婦人教育会館)　12　'85. 9　p 18　[0565]
◎参考文献　「女性の生き方と今後のライフコース設計」総合研究開発機構(NIRA OUTPUT)　'85. 11　p 345—353　　　　　　　　　　　　　[0566]
◎参考書　「日本女性文化史」(五十嵐富夫著)　吾妻館　'84. 5　p 254—257　　　　　　　　　　　　　　　　　　　　　　　　　　　　　　　[0567]
◎占領下の日本婦人政策関係年表，主な参考文献　「占領下の日本婦人政策　その歴史と証言」(西清子編著)　ドメス出版　'85. 8　p 221—230　[0568]

Sample Page of Shoshi nenkan

(Hint for Problem V-1: You are looking for a specialized bibliography. Since the language is not specified, you can start with Sheehy and its supplement or Walford. But you should also check *Nihon no sankō tosho: Kaisetsu sōran* and the other guides mentioned.)

(Hint for Problem V-2: You will need to check statistical sources, such as an index of Japanese statistics, and also a biographical dictionary or encyclopedia of Japanese literature, or newspaper indexes, in order to identify the year Kawabata Yasunari committed suicide.)

Quiz V-1. What type of articles appear in *Shigarami zōshi* しがらみ草紙? (Hint: This is a question concerning the characteristics of a journal. Since this type of information is usually not available in the directory of Japanese journals, you will have to find a specific tool to answer this question, unless, of course, your library has that particular journal. Start with what *Shigarami zōshi* is.)

IMPORTANT GUIDES TO REFERENCE WORKS DISCUSSED IN THIS CHAPTER

V-1. Sheehy, Eugene P. *Guide to Reference Books*, 10th ed. Chicago: American Library Association, 1986. xiv, 1560p.

V-2. Balay, Richard. *Guide to Reference Books: Covering Materials from 1985–1990*. Chicago: American Library Association, 1992. x, 613p. Supplement to V-1.

V-3. Walford, A. J. *Walford's Guide to Reference Materials*, 5th ed. New York: K. G. Saur, 1989.

V-4. *Nihon no sankō tosho: Kaisetsu sōran*. Tokyo: Nihon Toshokan Kyōkai, 1980. 907p. Updated by *Saikin no sankō tosho 1981–82* and *Nihon no sankō tosho: Shikiban* (Tokyo: Nihon Toshokan Kyōkai, 1985.

V-5. Fukuda, Naomi. *Bibliography of Reference Works for Japanese Studies*. Ann Arbor: Center for Japanese Studies, University of Michigan, 1979. ix, 210p.

V-6. *A Guide to Reference Books for Japanese Studies: Nihon kenkyū no tame no sankō tosho*. Tokyo: The International House of Japan Library, 1989. xii, 156p.

Chapter Six
Personal Names, Biographies, and Genealogies

So far, we have learned about the reference books such as bibliographies, indexes, and catalogs that we would need for a bibliographic search, particularly a retrospective one, of various topics. We have learned what to use and how to use them. In this section, we are going to discuss names we might come across while conducting our bibliographic search.

Japanese names, both surnames and given names, cause many problems, not only for foreigners, but also for native Japanese.[1] One of the biggest problems is the vast number of names, and another is the arbitrary and capricious nature of the readings. For example, how would you read 東海林? It can be read as either Tōkairin or Shōji. Instead of reading a compound in either the *on* or the *kun* reading, in some compounds one character is read in *on*, and the other in *kun*, or vice versa. There are even names for these types of confusing readings: one is *yutōyomi* 湯桶読み (*kun* plus *on*), and the other is *jūbakoyomi* 重箱読み (*on* plus *kun*). Including these different ways of reading, there are approximately 120,000 family names currently in use in Japan, as opposed to about 500 in China and about 270 in Korea.

Surnames have existed in Japan since the seventh century, when a surname was given to everyone except slaves for the purpose of census registration. Prior to that time, most people did not have surnames, and only the powerful clans had *kabane* 姓, a type of surname or hereditary title to show social and political status and

---

1. See Herschel Webb, *Research in Japanese Sources: A Guide* (New York: Published for the East Asian Institute, Columbia University, by Columbia University Press, 1965), 41–53, for a discussion of the problems that exist.

rank. *Kabane* were combined with given names. People in paternal blood-related groups called *uji* 氏 also had names to differentiate themselves from other groups. During the Nara period, even farmers had surnames, and slaves were the only people without them.[2] In the middle of the Heian period, the government stopped preparing census registers, and many of the common people stopped using surnames. Even the higher classes were identified by the names of the geographical locations of their residences, their first names, or the order of their birth among their siblings because too many people came to have the same family names, particularly among the most powerful four clans, Gen-Pei-Tō-Kitsu, namely, the Minamoto 源, Taira 平, Fujiwara 藤原, and Tachibana 橘. Because of this, family names lost their meaning and their indication of status, and given names became more important for identification or differentiation. An example of such a name is Ise no Saburō 伊勢の三郎, the third son of the one who resides in Ise. By the middle of the Muromachi period, it was illegal for farmers to use surnames.

During the Edo period, farmers and members of the merchant class were forbidden to use surnames, and the use of surnames became the privilege of aristocrats, the samurai class, physicians, and Shinto priests. Buddhist priests were not allowed to have surnames since they were considered to have forsaken the world. Among the nobility, only the emperors, empresses, and those of their children who were not allowed to found families of their own had no surnames. Sometimes surnames were even used to reward a member of the merchant class for a large donation to the local or central government. This use of a surname as reward became more common as the financial status of the ruling samurai class became weaker. It was called *myōji taitō*: "allowed to have a surname as well as to carry swords and to wear *kamishimo*," the old ceremonial, two-piece dress for men. When the Meiji government allowed commoners to have surnames in 1870, many people did not come forward to register their names, fearing some possible punishment. Thus, in 1875 the government reissued the order and required everyone to have surnames for registration and tax purposes. Many people had forgotten what their surnames had been and adapted the surnames that had long been in use.

2. Abe Takehiko, *Uji kabane* (1960), 130.

CHAPTER SIX

Another problem with Japanese surnames is that sometimes there is more than one reading for a surname written in the same way. For example, 角谷 could be read "Kadotani," "Kadoya," "Kadogai," "Sumiya," "Sumitani," "Kakutani," "Kakudani," "Kakuya," "Tsunotani," or "Tsunoya." Sometimes the same name is read differently for people from different areas of the country. For instance, in the eastern part of Japan, 古谷 is read "Furuya," and 西谷 is "Nishiya," but in the western part of Japan the same characters are read "Furutani" and "Nishitani," respectively.

A related problem is that the same name can be written with different characters. For instance, "Sakai" can be written as 堺, 境, 阪井, 坂井, and 酒井, or in another thirty-three different combinations. Also, surnames with the same pronunciation can be written in more than one way in characters. Saitō, for example, is written in more than thirty different ways based on the combination of such characters as 斉 西 細 斎 在 際 and 藤 東 桃 塔 堂 頭 当. The problem with given names is even worse than that with surnames because parents can assign almost any reading they wish to the characters of their choice. Even mistakenly assigned readings become legitimate once registered: for example, note the readings of the Chinese character 一 , which means "one," in O'Neill's *Japanese Names*.

Recognizing a string of Chinese characters as a person's name is sometimes problematic, especially in a text without word division. Consider the following example. 委員長谷川俊助教授 is ambiguous. This string of Chinese characters can be read in at least four different ways, not to mention possible alternate readings: Committee Chairman Professor Tanigawa Shunsuke, Committee Chairman Assistant Professor Tanigawa Shun, Committee member Professor Hasegawa Shunsuke, or Committee member Assistant Professor Hasegawa Shun.

Another problem is the number of names used for the same person. Until forbidden by law in 1872, people of the samurai and higher classes used both given names and names by which they were commonly known. Besides given names, there are *yōmei* 幼名 or *tsūshō* 通称, "aliases" or "popularly known names"; *azana* 字 , such as [林] 子信, which were commonly used among scholars and literary men; and *gō* 号, a "sobriquet." For the samurai class, *yōmei*, "childhood names," were used until a boy's *genpuku* ceremony at the age of thirteen. For example, Shogun Tokugawa Ieyasu was called Takechiyo when he was a child. Matsuo Bashō's real name was

Matsuo Munefusa, and Bashō was only one of his many pseudonyms, among which were Kinsaku, Tadazaemon, Tadaemon, Tōsei, Mumeian, and Yōkaku. Kyokutei Bakin, a popular author in the Edo period, was said to have used thirty-five different names. Holding multiple names, such as Saigō Kichinosuke Takamori, was forbidden by law in 1872, but even after that, using pseudonyms was perfectly legitimate. Many people, particularly literary figures, scholars, and artists, continued to use multiple pseudonyms. The general rule used for handling names in a library is to file each person by his or her most popular and widely known name, to which see-references are provided. For researchers, however, secondary names are also of importance. For example, Mishima Yukio wrote some of his early works under his real name, Hiraoka Kimitake. In 1984, two of Mishima's unpublished works written under Hiraoka were found in a university library in Tokyo.

1. READINGS AND WRITINGS

Problem VI-1. What is the standard reading of the surname 利谷, whose article I read recently?

For finding the readings or writings of names in general, consult O'Neill's *Japanese Names: A Comprehensive Index by Characters and Readings* (VI-1). This book is very easy to use and convenient for speakers of English, and includes both personal and geographical Japanese names. Entries are arranged in two sections: the first section is by the stroke count of Chinese characters, and the second section is by alphabetical order of the readings of the names. It also includes a radical index. When you cannot find names in this handy dictionary, it is necessary to use Japanese-language sources. *Nihon seishi daijiten* 日本姓氏大事典 (VI-2), which includes over 130,000 family names, consists of a volume arranged by *hyōki hen* 表記編 (stroke count of the first character), a volume arranged in *hyōon hen* 表音編 (Japanese syllabary order), and an explanatory volume. This is the revised edition of *Nihon no myōji*. The names are classified into thirty-three types by origin, such as occupational, geographical, Ainu, and foreign. *Hyōki hen* can be used to find the readings of names, while *hyōon hen* is useful for learning the possible ways of writing certain surnames.

Jinmei yomikata jiten 人名よみかた辞典 (VI-3) is a two-volume dictionary of Japanese personal names and surnames that have been collected from sources that have appeared since 1868. One volume is devoted to surnames, and the other to personal names. Both volumes are arranged by the radical of the first character of each name, and examples of the names of real people are given with reading, profession, and the source of biographical information. Indexes are arranged by the pronunciation of Chinese characters, both *on* 音 and *kun* 訓 readings, and by radicals. *Rekishi jinmei yomikata jiten* 歴史人名よみかた辞典 (VI-4) includes 40,000 Japanese historical figures from ancient times (including the names of gods and goddesses) to the end of the Edo period arranged by the reading of the first character. Information that is given includes the name in Chinese characters, the reading in *hiragana*, the romanized name, dates, occupation or position, and the source of the data. When more than one reading of the name exists, these are included along with the source of information. It contains an index arranged by Japanese syllabary, an *on-kun* reading guide, and a stroke-count order guide.

(Hint for Problem VI-1: The key point of this problem is to find the common reading of a surname, not the specific reading of a specific person's name.)

Problem VI-2. Who is Geite ゲーテ?

There are a few reference tools for reading and finding the original spellings of the names of Westerners. *Seiyō jinmei yomikata jiten* 西洋人名よみかた辞典 (VI-5) includes readings and original spellings of 60,000 Western names in various subject areas. Each entry leads to a biographical dictionary and also includes a short biography of the person, including dates and occupation. It is convenient for finding the original spelling of a name from *kana* or the Japanized reading of a name. *Chū-Nichi-Ō taishō sekai chimei jinmei jiten* 中日欧世界地名人名辞典 (VI-6) and *Kan'yaku Kanmei Seiyō jinmei jiten* 漢訳漢名西洋人名辞典 are used to identify Westerners whose names have been written in Chinese. Stroke-count indexes enable the users to find the original spelling of the name.

Problem VI-3. The given name 松前健, the author of *Nihon shinwa no keisei* 日本神話の形成, is read differently from source to source as "Ken," "Takeshi," and "Tsuyoshi." What is the correct reading?

When you are looking for the specific reading of the name of an author of a book, you can check *Kokuritsu Kokkai Toshokan choshamei tenkyoroku* 国立国会図書館著者名典拠録 (VI-7). This is an authority list of over 200,000 Japanese authors since 1868 whose work has been cataloged by the National Diet Library since its opening in 1948. The volumes cover the period up to the end of March 1991, and there is an index volume arranged by the stroke count of the first Chinese character of the name. Information includes the writing of the name in Japanese, dates, profession or affiliation, title of the book, notes, sources for establishing authority, and references.

Another way of checking authors includes looking in *Gendai Nihon shippitsusha daijiten* 現代日本執筆者大事典 (VI-8) and *Nihon jinmei tenkyoroku* 日本人名典拠録, which is the general index of *Jinbutsu refarensu jiten* (VI-25), which we will discuss in section 4 of this chapter. *Nihon jinmei tenkyoroku* is very easy to use and is an extremely useful tool for our purposes here. Since it covers 180,000 Japanese names from ancient times to the present, it can be used as an efficient directory to find the correct reading of a specific person's name. The index volume of *Daijinmei jiten / Nihon jinmei daijiten* (VI-16) also serves our purpose of finding the reading of a name. It has a Chinese-character index arranged by stroke count.

When the title of a book is known but the correct reading of the author's name is not known, use *Shomei sakuin* 書名索引 (title index) of *Nihon choshamei sōmokuroku* 日本著者名総目録 (Tokyo: Nichigai Asoshieitsu, 1987–). Although it is extremely expensive and not many libraries in the United States are likely to own the whole set (it covers publications since 1945), if your library has it, use it. The names of authors and translators are arranged in Japanese syllabary order, so to use the main volumes, you must have some idea of how to read the last name. Due to the lack of a Chinese-character index for the author's name, this expensive and extensive work is limited in its usefulness. For finding the reading of an author's name, you have to know the title of a book; otherwise, you have to be able to accurately guess how to read the name.

(Hint for Problem VI-3: This is asking for the specific reading of the author's name.)

Quiz VI-1. What is the Chinese character for the first name of Inoue Kōji, who is the compiler of *Zusetsu Nihon no rekishi* 図説日本の歴史, published in eighteen volumes by Shūeisha?

58   CHAPTER SIX

2. WHO'S WHO

Problem VI-4. I want to translate a book written by Haga Kōshirō 芳賀幸四郎 . What is his address? What is his place of work?

Although it is not very good, *Who's Who in Japan,* published in Hong Kong since 1984, is the most recent extensive book of its type in English on Japanese personalities. *Gendai Nihon jinmeiroku* 現代日本人名録 (VI-9) is unique in covering extremely broad subject areas, from explorers to the prime minister. It includes numerous Japanese currently active, many of whom would not be found in standard works such as *Jinji kōshinroku* or *Sankei Nihon shinshi nenkan.* The information that appears in *Gendai Nihon jinmeiroku* includes an individual's name and its reading and the individual's occupation, speciality, nationality, date and place of birth, real name or pseudonym, education, interests and accomplishments, prizes, affiliation, family, place of work (address and phone included), home address, and telephone number. The work is frequently updated.

Jinji kōshinroku 人事興信録 (VI-10), which corresponds to *Who's Who,* is the most comprehensive work of this kind. It lists brief biographical information arranged in Japanese syllabary order for over 100,000 prominent living Japanese. Individuals from a wide variety of occupations—politicians, government officials, professors, company executives, physicians, novelists, and media personalities—are listed. The information provided includes the name and its reading, place of birth, profession or position, place where the person is registered, family, education, career, accomplishments, publications, hobby, religion, siblings, relatives, friends, address, telephone number, place of work, and other such information. Nobility and the imperial family are listed separately at the beginning of the volume. It is published every other year. Other similar, authoritative works include *Nihon shinshiroku* 日本紳士録 (VI-11) and *Sankei Nihon shinshi nenkan* 産経日本紳士年鑑 (VI-12).

Problem VI-5. What is the full name of Takano, the author of *Nihon kayōshi* 日本歌謡史 ?

Gendai Nihon shippitsusha daijiten, mentioned above, is an excellent who's who if the person in question is a writer. It includes not only those who write books but also those who only write articles, as well as interviews and informal talks in all fields except natural sciences. The reading of the name, brief biographical information, association memberships, a list of publications, and biographical studies appear for each person listed. Recently published works about the individual are also included. Index volumes contain a subject index and a pseudonym and stage name index.

Chosakuken daichō: Bunkajin meiroku 著作権台帳：文化人名録 (VI-13), a directory of copyright holders, also has other uses. It lists authors, artists, and performers in the area of the arts and includes information such as personal name, reading of the name, real name, pseudonym, pen names, birthplace, dates, address, telephone number, subject field, alma mater, major and year of graduation from college, degree earned, prizes, previous jobs, membership in associations, publications, translations, and related information. It can be useful when you do not know the reading of a surname or a first name, or, for example, when you must look up someone for translation rights. However, sections in some editions are often excluded; you are then referred to those sections in an earlier edition.

(Hint for Problem VI-5: *Bunkajin meiroku* is divided by subject area, and you have to make a good guess to find the answer to this question. You can also use other reference books.)

If there is a directory of researchers in your field, it should be consulted. For instance, for government officials after 1885, consult *Shokuinroku* 職員録 (VI-14). It lists government officials from the lowest to the highest under their local or national organization. It is arranged by institution and includes address, telephone number, job title, and the person's name. A name index for both volumes is included in volume 2. You can trace government officials back to the Heian period using the forerunners of *Shokuinroku* such as *Kugyō bunin* 公卿補任 or *Daibukan* 大武鑑. One of the most convenient and up-to-date directories for contemporary names and institutions is the directory in the supplement of *nenkan* 年鑑, published by major newspapers such as *Asahi nenkan* 朝日年鑑.

Kenkyūsha kenkyū kadai sōran: Jinbun shakai kagaku hen 研究者研究課題総覧...人文社会科学篇 (VI-15) is designed to facilitate the exchange of information in the fields of the humanities and

石原慎太郎

衆議院議員（自民・東京二・圓⑥）作家 日本の新しい世代の会会長 日本外洋帆走協会会長

母 光子 明42、9、6生
妻 典子 昭13、1、1生
長男 伸晃 昭32、4、19生、慶大文学部卒
二男 良純 昭37、6、15生、慶応高校卒
三男 宏高 昭39、8、16生、慶応高校卒
四男 延啓 昭41、22生、慶応高校卒

昭和7年9月30日生る同31年一橋大法学部卒業在学中より小説を発表文学界新人賞を受け「太陽の季節」により昭和31年度芥川賞を受賞文壇に認められ同46年3月「化石の森」により第21回芸術選奨文部大臣賞を受け更にシナリオ執筆映画出演同監督等にも進出す主なる作品は「理由なき復讐」「狂った果実」「北壁」「青春にあるもの」として「青年の樹」「挑戦」「汚れた夜」「亀裂」「日本零年」「孤独なる戴冠」「怒りの像」評論「プレイボーイの哲学」「野蛮人のネクタイ」「スパルタ教育」「大人をサラリーマンにしない法」「光より速く我ら」等あり同34年7月自民党に入党同42年9月南米に旅行同43年7月参議院議員に当選同47年12月以来衆議院議員に6回当選同51年12月福田内閣の国務大臣環境庁長官に就任司52年11月退任司52年11月竹下

千葉県市川市広尾二丁目三一一☎(○四七三) 57 272-01
分ニ丁目一六一三☎(○四七三) 71 2260七圓
一八一

石原 靖三

長 石原工業㈱顧問 東京中小企業国友会名誉会員 日本AALA連体委員会常任理事
東京都出身
妻 笹子 大13 3女卒、東京、猪瀬謙二女、府立三女卒
長女 由起子 昭22、1生
長男 義久 昭24、6、1生
二女 多佳子 昭26、12、12生
二男 満久 昭30、1生

大正5年6月1日長崎県故関東ゴム調帯会長脩吉の二男に生る昭和16年慶大経済科卒業関東ゴム調帯石原開発興業各専務を歴任す 國読書ハイキング 園日蓮宗圓兄煕造(大2 7 20生、早大電気工学科卒、石原鋼鉄社長)弟令雄(慶大経済科卒、三菱商事勤務)弟新三(学習院大卒、北海道ゴム工業所社長)

圍東京都小平市上水本町一五六八番地六一一〇
五☎(○四二三)24三七五八

Sample page of Jinji kōshinroku

social sciences among researchers and scholars in Japanese colleges, technical colleges, universities, and other research institutions (a companion to this book covers the sciences). It is divided by discipline and contains cross-references to the researchers' minor fields. Entries are arranged in Japanese syllabary order. Entries include the researcher's name, reading of the name, current position, alma mater, degrees earned, memberships in associations and societies, current research topics (up to three), and major publications and dates of major events. Foreigners are listed in alphabetical order at the end of each field. An appendix contains a list of all the institutions mentioned in the entries, with their addresses and phone numbers. A name index is combined with the social science volume and is arranged in Japanese syllabary order by institution. Supplement editions were published and include new entries and changes.

Quiz VI-2. I am looking for a personal critique of Ishimure Michiko 石牟礼道子. Where should I look?

Quiz VI-3. What is the real name of Saotome Mitsugu 早乙女貢, the author of the novel *Okei* おけい?

3. BIOGRAPHICAL DICTIONARIES

Although the language is rather old-fashioned and difficult for beginners to use, *Daijinmei jiten/Nihon jinmei daijiten* 大人名事典/日本人名大事典 (VI-16) is the standard, authoritative biographical dictionary in Japan. The first six volumes cover 50,000 Japanese historical figures, volumes 7 and 8 cover over 10,000 foreigners, and volume 9 covers 8,000 contemporary (at the time of compilation in 1953) Japanese. When a person is known equally well under different names, there is a cross-reference. When the dates are disputed, that fact is stated. An index of Japanese names (surnames, given names, and pen names) arranged in Japanese syllabary order and by stroke count and an alphabetical index for foreigners are included in volume 10. A major part of this dictionary was reprinted in 1979 under the title *Nihon jinmei daijiten,* supplemented with a volume called *Gendai.* This volume title is misleading because this supplemental volume includes 6,000 Japanese who died between

1.3 史　　学

1.3.1 日本史

本の存在形態―鴻池，小西屋を例として―". 大阪商業大学論集. (62), (1981).

安藤　保　ANDO, Tamotsu (1941. 8. 18) 鹿児島大・教育・教授　⑬九大・文／九大・博・文・国史　⑫文修　⑭社会経済史学会，歴史学研究会，九州史学研究会　⑰地域的金融市場の発達と藩財政　⑱"嘉永期福岡藩における財政の諸策". 九州文化史研究所紀要. (30), (1985). "嘉永安政期における福岡藩の財政と広瀬久兵衛". 『福岡県史』近世研究編福岡藩(三), (1988). "薩摩藩城下士の生活と意識". 『西南地域の史的展開』近世篇, (1988).

安藤英男　ANDO, Hideo (1927. 1. 5) 国士舘大・武道徳育研・助教授　⑬法政大・経済・経済学(貨幣論)　⑫文博　⑭蘇峰会賞　⑮法政大学史学会　⑰明治6年政変の研究(起因と，その影響)／天誅組の研究(その結成，行動，意義)／頼山陽と経学(特に朱子学との関わり)　⑱"雲井龍雄研究3部作(5冊)(自1961至1981(評伝発掘考証)". 光風社出版(有), (1981). "頼山陽全書全7巻(7冊)(自1981至1982". (有)近藤出版社, (1982). "蒲生君平山陵志(『山陵志』解題と完釈)". (有)りくえつ, (1979).

安藤正人　ANDO, Masahito 国文学研究資料館・助手 ⇨ 8.0.2 情報学

安藤良平　ANDO, Ryohei (1920. 5. 20) 跡見学園女大・文・教授　⑬東京帝国大・人文科・国史　⑭日本歴史学会，日本古文書学会　⑰国事鞅掌者の映像第四部　⑱"国事鞅掌者の映像". 雄文社. 1, (1960). "近世史論攷". 望月印刷出版社. 1, (1962).

September 1938 and August 1978. The justification for this is that the first six volumes included people who had been dead by August 1938. As a result of this, for contemporary people, users still should consult *Gendai hen* of *Daijinmei jiten* (volume 9), and not *Nihon jinmei daijiten: Gendai,* although the publication date of the latter is a quarter of a century later.

Problem VI-6. How do you pronounce 維斎 and who is he?

It has been a custom in Japan from ancient times to call famous people by their first names. Who is Norinaga, or Yoshimoto, or Tsurayuki? You probably know or have heard about them. Unfortunately, as a general rule biographical dictionaries presuppose a knowledge of surnames. It is next to impossible to find people without knowing the surname, unless they are monks or nuns. We do not have to go back to the premodern period to find examples. Even after the Meiji era, there are a fair number of people who do not use surnames. This practice is particularly common among poets, literary authors, or artists. For many years, *Nihon jinmei jiten* 日本人名辞典 by Haga Yaichi served as a resource for finding information on such people. Now we have *Namae kara hiku jinmei jiten* 名前から引く人名辞典 (VI-17), a first-name dictionary of Japanese people, from ancient times to the present, who are often remembered by their given names, studio names, or pseudonyms. *Nihon jinmei jiten* is still useful for identifying first names such as *nanori* 名乗, *tsūshō* 通称, *gagō* 雅号, and *geimei* 芸名.

Problem VI-7. Check the birth and death dates of Ōwada Tateki 大和田建樹 in three different biographical dictionaries.

Problem VI-8. Is the first name of 市村羽左衛門 "Hanezaemon"?

Meiji kakochō: Bukko jinmei jiten shinteiban 明治過去帳 (VI-18) is a listing of brief biographical entries for over 20,000 people who died during the Meiji era. Names were collected from newspapers, *kanpō* (official gazettes), and graves. It was originally published under the title *Kokumin kakochō: Meiji no maki* in 1935. *Taishō kakochō: Bukko jinmei jiten* 大正過去帳 (VI-19), following the same format, covers approximately 4,000 people who died during the

Taishō era. For the Shōwa era, there are *Shōwa bukko jinmeiroku 1926–1979* 昭和物故人名録 (VI-20), *Gendai bukkosha jiten 1980–1982* 現代物故者事典 (VI-21), and *Japan Who Was Who: Bukkosha jiten 1983–1987* 物故者事典 (VI-22).

There are numerous other biographical dictionaries in specific subject areas in both English and Japanese. *A Dictionary of Japanese Artists* by Laurence P. Roberts (New York: Weatherhill, 1976; xi, 299p.), *Biographical Dictionary of Japanese History* edited by Seiichi Iwao, translated by Burton Watson (Tokyo: Kodansha International in collaboration with the International Society for Educational Information, 1978; 655p.), and *Biographical Dictionary of Japanese Literature* by Sen'ichi Hisamatsu (Tokyo: International Society for Educational Information, 1976; 437p.) are a few of the examples in English. Besides general biographical dictionaries, there are numerous types of special biographical dictionaries that are based on regions, historical periods, or various subjects, such as women, gods and goddesses, invented names, literature, and art. For a specific subject area, consult *Nihon no sankō tosho: Kaisetsu sōran,* discussed in chapter five "Guides to Reference Tools."

Besides biographical dictionaries in each subject area, subject dictionaries and subject encyclopedias are excellent sources of biographical information. *Nihon Kindai Bungaku daijiten* 日本近代文学大事典, *Engeki hyakka daijiten* 演劇百科大辞典, *Tetsugaku jiten* 哲学辞典, and *The Kodansha Encyclopedia of Japan* are some examples. *Dai Nihon josei jinmei jisho* 大日本女性人名辞書 is one of the special biographical dictionaries, and the first biographical dictionary of Japanese women written by one of the pioneers of Japanese feminist scholarship, Takamure Itsue 高群逸枝. It was first published in 1936 and includes over 2,000 real, legendary, and mythological Japanese women who appeared in various historical sources and died by the 1930s. *Nihon josei jinmei jiten* 日本女性人名辞典, which includes material on approximately 7,000 women from ancient to modern times in various fields, will replace Takamure's work. The inclusion of bibliographic material on the sources will extend its usefulness for future research.

Problem VI-9. I am studying the origin of the concept of individualism in Japan. The names Rudorufu Busse ルドルフ ブッセ and Ji Uiriamu Nokkusu ジ ウイリアム ノックス come up frequently in various sources. I believe both of them were foreign teachers at

Imperial University. Who were they? Did they publish any articles or books?

Foreigners' names pose a unique problem. Japanese tends to Japanize their pronunciation, which often makes it difficult to guess the original pronunciations or spellings. Consult *Iwanami Seiyō jinmei jiten* 岩波西洋人名辞典 (VI-23) in such cases. Approximately 25,000 foreign names, including European, American, Middle and Near Eastern, African, Oceanian, and Indian, both historical and current, are listed. It focuses on the people who have had strong ties to China and Japan. Information given includes the original spelling of the name, dates, biographical data, and publications when applicable. It has both alphabetical and Chinese character indexes. The user must be alert to the fact that the supplemental portion for this enlarged edition is not incorporated into the main text.

Rainichi Seiyō jinmei jiten 来日西洋人名辞典 (VI-24) is another useful biographical dictionary for Japanese studies in particular. This unique reference work includes information on 1,133 Westerners who lived in Japan between 1544 and 1942 for varying lengths of time and who contributed to the modernization of Japan and its people. Most of the subjects arrived in Japan after the opening of the country. Their fields of speciality cover all areas, from foreign relations to sports. The entries are arranged in Japanese syllabary order according to the most commonly known Japanese pronunciation of the name. The original spelling of the name is followed by dates, nationality, specific area of the person's activities, and biographical information. Bibliography is listed for each entry. There are indexes of names, one arranged by profession and one in alphabetical order of original spelling. An appendix contains a chronological table of each person's year of arrival in Japan.

4. PERSONAL NAME INDEXES

Problem VI-10. Who is Hirakata Kingorō 枚方金五郎? Is there any biographical information about him? He is not listed in *Nihon jinmei daijiten*.

Jinbutsu refarensu jiten 人物レファレンス事典 (VI-25) is extremely useful when you are looking for biographical data. It is an extensive index to biographical sources from ancient times to the present. It is arranged by period and guides the user to various dictionaries, encyclopedias, and biographical dictionaries and directories. Its seven volumes are divided into four parts: Part 1, *Kodai, chūsei hen* 古代中世編 ; Part 2, *Kinsei hen* 近世編 ; Part 3, *Gendai hen* 現代編 ; and Part 4, *Nihon jinmei tenkyoroku* 日本人名典拠録.

This index to the biographical information sources of thirty-seven biographical and special dictionaries and other works supplies information on where you can find biographical information. It also provides brief biographical information, such as the reading of the name, dates, occupation, and birthplace for approximately 180,000 people from ancient times to the present, which itself is sufficient in many cases and eliminates the need for a further search. Part 4 also serves as the index to the first three parts and, being arranged by the first Chinese character of the surname, could be consulted in the same way as a Chinese character dictionary. There are indexes arranged by readings, by radicals, and by stroke counts. Each entry in part 4 is arranged by radical and includes the readings of the name, dates, profession, and where in the first three parts the biographical information for that entry can be found. The extent of biographical information in the source is indicated by an arrow and the number of asterisks for parts 1-3. The first three parts are arranged in Japanese syllabary order and include Chinese characters, readings, brief information, and biographical sources. A stroke-count index table is supplied for finding the readings.

Seiyō jinbutsu refarensu jiten 西洋人物レファレンス事典 is a sequel to *Jinbutsu refarensu jiten* (VI-25). This extensive biographical dictionary, a compilation of thirty-eight dictionaries, lists 150,000 people, including Japanese, Chinese, and nationals of other Asian countries, who have been active in other countries. It is divided into *Kodai chūsei hen, Kinsei hen, Gendai hen,* and *Seiyō jinmei tenkyoroku.* This fourth section can be used as general index to the first three parts. Indexes are arranged in alphabetical order of the original spelling of the names, and in Japanese syllabary order. It is extremely useful. *Tōyō jinbutsu refarensu jiten* 東洋人物レファレンス事典 covers China, Korea, and Southeast Asia, including minority groups around China.

(Hint for Problem VI-10: When no information is available in regular biographical dictionaries, *Jinbutsu refarensu jiten* is the perfect re-

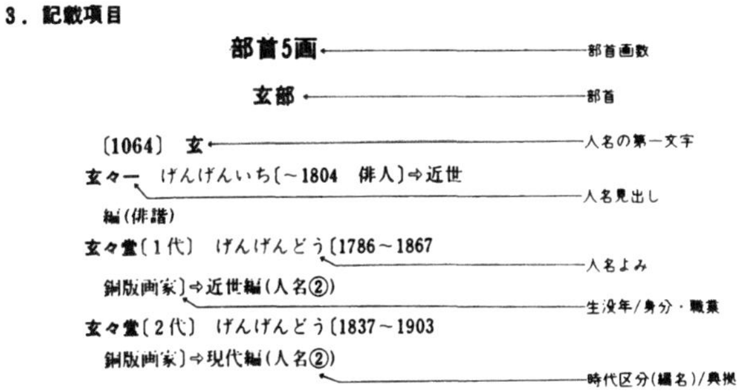
3．記載項目
部首5画
部首画数
玄部
部首
〔1064〕 玄
人名の第一文字
玄々一 げんげんいち〔～1804 俳人〕⇨近世
人名見出し
編（俳諧）
玄々堂〔1代〕 げんげんどう〔1786～1867
人名よみ
銅版画家〕⇨近世編（人名②）
生没年／身分・職業
玄々堂〔2代〕 げんげんどう〔1837～1903
銅版画家〕⇨現代編（人名②）
時代区分（編名）／典拠

平方金五郎　ひらかたきんごろう〔1834～1867　水戸藩士〕⇨近世編(維新)

平木一　ひらきいつ〔1919～　宇宙開発事業団理事〕⇨現代編(人情③)

平木二六　ひらきにろく〔1903～　詩人〕⇨現代編(文学)

平賀晋民　ひらがしんみん
1722～1792　徳川中期の儒者。通称孫次郎、惣右衛門、名は叔明のちに晋民、中南、果亭と号す。㊓安芸豊田郡忠海。
⇨**人名⑤；*コン(1721～1792)

平方金五郎　ひらかたきんごろう
1834～1867　水戸藩士。㊓常陸国。
⇨*維新

Sample page of Jinbutsu refarensu jiten

source for finding where the information for the person, if Japanese, can be located.)

5. BIOGRAPHIES

Problem VI-11. Where can I find an authoritative biography of Izawa Shuji 伊沢修二?

When you are looking for detailed information beyond what you can find in biographical dictionaries, *Jinbutsu sōsho* 人物叢書 (VI-26) is an excellent source. Each volume in this series is devoted to a single person and is written by a specialist on that person. There are many individual biographies available, and thus check under the subject's name in bibliographies or in the card catalogs of libraries. Although there are many other monographic series similar to *Jinbutsu sōsho,* probably none is as extensive and authoritative. *Nihonjin no jiden* 日本人の自伝 and *Watakushi no rirekisho* 私の履歴書 are two of the other biographical series.

(Hint for Problem VI-11: Go to *Jinbutsu sōsho,* which is written by specialists.)

6. GENEALOGIES

Problem VI-12. I want to find the roots of the Muroga 室賀 family, whose origin can be traced to the Sengoku era. I understand that they originated near Komoro, Nagano Prefecture.

Seishi kakei daijiten 姓氏家系大事典 (VI-27), an etymological dictionary of Japanese surnames collected exhaustively from pre-1868 books, documents, and records, explains the origin of a family, its lineage, and the distribution of surnames. When families with the same name have different origins, all are enumerated. Arranged in Japanese syllabary order, *Seishi kakei daijiten* often includes citations and family crests. Genealogical tables of mythological gods and the imperial family are included at the beginning of volume 1. For other specific, prominent aristocratic families before the Meiji era, check *Sonpi bunmyaku* 尊卑分脈 (in *Shintei zōho Kokushi taikei*, which covers surnames up to the beginning of the Muromachi period), *Gunsho keizubushū* 群書系図部集 (in *Gunsho ruijū* and *Zoku Gunsho ruijū*), or *Kansei chōshū shokafu* 寛政重修諸家譜.

Nihon keifu sōran 日本系譜綜覧 (VI-28) is a collection of Japanese genealogical tables of the imperial family, Korean kings, courtiers, military families, Buddhist sects, major scholarly institutions, art and craft schools, martial arts schools, and more. It was published in 1936 and reprinted in 1973. The book has an appendix of various tables but contains no index. *Keizu bunken shiryō sōran* 系図文献資料総覧 (VI-29) is an extensive handbook of genealogical studies. It is divided into eight parts: part 1 contains basic sources; 2, bibliography; 3, related materials; 4, a catalog of documents and records related to genealogy owned by public libraries and other institutions, arranged by the holding institutions; and 5, genealogical studies published in the form of monographs or journal articles arranged by family name in Japanese syllabary order. Parts 6 and 7 are supplements to parts 1 and 2; part 8 is a series of bibliographies of families who are arranged in Japanese syllabary order.

There is an extensive introductory work for genealogical studies called *Keizu kenkyū no kiso chishiki: Kakei ni miru Nihon ne rekishi* 系図研究の基礎知識 (VI-30).

7. PERSONAL BIBLIOGRAPHIES

Problem VI-13. I am looking for materials written about Enchi Fumiko 円地文子. Where should I start my search?

Nihon jinbutsu bunken mokuroku 日本人物文献目録 (VI-31) includes publications on over 30,000 Japanese that appeared from 1868 to 1966 in the form of monographs, journal articles, and even mimeographs. The arrangement is under the well-known form of the subject's name with good cross-references in Japanese syllabary order. Entries for each subject are grouped into bibliography, monographs, and serial publications. An appendix lists the sources consulted. It is a useful guide when beginning the search for materials about a particular individual.

Jinbutsu shoshi sakuin 人物書誌索引 (VI-32) continues the above work and indexes 8,000 items on 4,200 people, both Japanese and foreigners. The items were published in Japan from 1966 through 1977, mainly in books and journals. People indexed in *Jinbutsu bunken sakuin* 人物文献索引 (VI-33), compiled by the National Diet Library, and *Nihon jinbutsu bunken mokuroku* were excluded from this index, so it should be used along with them. The arrangement is in Japanese syllabary order, and when one person appears under more than one name, the form in which the name appears more often is used as the entry word, with cross-references to the other forms. *Nenkan jinbutsu bunken mokuroku* 年刊人物文献目録 (VI-34) is the extension of the above work. This annual publication, which began in 1980, includes information on biographies collected from books and journals written in Japanese. Any biographies missed in earlier volumes are picked up in the current one. Unlike *Nihon jinbutsu bunken mokuroku,* this annual bibliography includes biographies of both Japanese and foreigners. In general, entries are under the person's real name, with some cross-references. Beginning with the 1981 edition it is divided into two parts: *Nihonjin hen* and *Gaikokujin hen.* For Japanese subjects, the name in Chinese characters is listed in Japanese syllabary order, and its reading is given. The title of the biography, its writer, the title and volume number of the journal, when applicable, the date of publication, and the series title, when applicable, are included. Volume 2, on foreigners, is also arranged in Japanese syllabary order according to the Japanese pronunciation of the subjects' names. It lists the original spelling of a person's name and contains the same information as the volume on Japanese subjects. The information is in Japanese in the case of Westerners, and in Chinese characters for Chinese and Koreans.

Nihon Toyo hen 日本東洋編, part 1 of *Denki, hyōden zenjōhō 45/89* 伝記評伝全情報 (VI-35), is a bibliography of 54,000 memoirs, diaries, biographies, collections of letters, and critical discussions of 18,000 Japanese, Chinese, and Korean authors who published books in Japan between 1945 and 1989. Authors of children's books were not included. The work is arranged by author according to Japanese syllabary order.

In addition to the above-mentioned collective personal bibliographies, Nichigai Associates has begun publishing *Jinbutsu shoshi taikei* 人物書誌大系 (VI-36), a series of personal bibliographies on individual authors, mainly in the field of Japanese literature.

Select several dictionaries and biographical dictionaries, such as *Daijinmei jiten, Sekai daihyakka jiten,* and *Nihon bungaku daijiten,*

4. 文献の排列と記載の形式
 1) 排列
   見出し語のもとに、書誌、図書、雑誌の順とし、各々の初めに◇・◎・○を付して識別した。複数の場合は、刊行年月順とした。
 2) 記載の形式
   下記の原則によって記載した。
   (1)図書
       ◎書名―副書名／（著編者等）／発行所／発行年月／（叢書名）
     (例)◎実業の詩人・岩崎弥太郎―三菱をつくった男（嶋岡晨）名著刊行会　昭60.1
   なお、論集・図書の一部分については以下のように記載した。
       ◎書名―副書名／（著編者等）／発行所／発行年月／（叢書名）／
       論題／（著者）
     (例)◎新編近代美人伝(下)　（長谷川時雨著，杉本苑子編）　岩波書店　昭60.12（岩波文庫）
         大塚楠緒子
   (2)雑誌の論文
       ○論題／（著編者）／：誌名／巻(号)／発行年月
     (例)○明治の雄　大隈重信（榛葉英治）：波　183　昭60.3
   なお、特集形式については以下のように記載した。
       ○特集名／：誌名／巻(号)／発行年月／
       論題／（著者）
     (例)○泉鏡花―魔界の精神史：国文学　30(7)　昭60.6
         境界線上の文学―鏡花世界の原郷（対談）(前田愛、山口昌男)
         幻想の文法学（野口武彦）
         鏡花の劇空間（郡司正勝）
   (3)書誌
     書誌（年譜、略歴、著作目録、参考文献類）については上記の記載形式によったが、冒頭に◇印を付してある。

遠藤周作　（えんどうしゅうさく*）
◎レトリックス―大衆文芸技術論―(渡部直己)　五月書房　昭60.6
　　〈伏線〉の誘惑―遠藤周作
◎「沈黙」以後―遠藤周作の世界(武田友寿)　女子パウロ会　昭60.6
○遠藤周作の作品「わたしが・棄てた・女」にみる「運命の連帯感」(大木マリア)：日本語日本文学(輔仁大学外語学院)　11　昭59.12
○遠藤周作文芸とキリスト教(細川正義)：九州女学院短期大学学術紀要　10　昭60.3
○遠藤周作論(5)(上総英郎)：論究(二松学舎大学)

Sample page of Nenkan jinbutsu bunken mokuroku

and compare the information about 下河辺長流. What are the readings of his name in each dictionary? What are his dates? How old was he when he died? The purpose of this exercise is to illustrate that not all the information is the same. Some sources read the characters as "Shimokōbe Nagaru," others as "Shimokōbe Chōryū," and yet others as "Shimokawabe" and "Shimokaube" (Rekishiteki kanazukai-Jion kanazukai). Some books give different dates, and some list a different age at the time of his death. We hope you will learn from this to be cautious when you look for biographical information. Make it a habit to use multiple dictionaries for biographical information. When in doubt, make a thorough search, particularly when you are using this information in a research paper, dissertation, or thesis.

IMPORTANT REFERENCE WORKS
ON JAPANESE NAMES DISCUSSED IN THIS CHAPTER

VI-1. O'Neill, P. G. *Japanese Names: A Comprehensive Index by Characters and Readings.* New York and Tokyo: John Weatherhill, 1972. xvi, 359p.

VI-2. Niwa Motoji. *Nihon seishi daijiten.* Tokyo: Kadokawa Shoten, 1985. 3v.

VI-3. *Jinmei yomikata jiten.* Tokyo: Nichigai Asoshieitsu, 1983. 2v.

VI-4. *Rekishi jinmei yomikata jiten.* Tokyo: Nichigai Asoshieitsu, 1989. 38, 1,221p.

VI-5. *Seiyō jinmei yomikata jiten.* Tokyo: Nichigai Asoshieitsu, 1984. 3v.

VI-6. Takenouchi Yasumi. *Chū-Nichi-Ō taishō sekai chimei jinmei jiten.* Tokyo: Kokusho Kankōkai, 1978. 477, 267p.

VI-7. Kokuritsu Kokkai Toshokan, ed. *Kokuritsu Kokkai Toshokan choshamei tenkyoroku: Meiji ikō Nihon jinmei,* 2d edition. Tokyo: Kokuritsu Kokkai Toshokan, 1991. 5v and index.

VI-8. *Gendai Nihon shippitsusha daijiten.* Tokyo: Nichigai Asoshieitsu, 1978. 5v. Then *Gendai Nihon shippitsusha daijiten, 77/82* (Tokyo:

Nichigai Asoshieitsu, 1984. 5v.) and *Shin gendai Nihon shippitsusha daijiten* (Tokyo: Nichigai Asoshieitsu, 1992–93. 5v.).

VI-9. *Gendai Nihon jinmeiroku.* Tokyo: Nichigai Asoshieitsu, 1987–.

VI-10. *Jinji kōshinroku.* Tokyo: Jinji Kōshinjo, 1903–.

VI-11. *Nihon shinshiroku.* Tokyo: Kōjunsha, 1889–.

VI-12. *Sankei Nihon shinshi nenkan.* Tokyo: Sankei Shinbunsha, 1958–.

VI-13. *Chosakuken daichō: Bunkajin meiroku.* Tokyo: Nihon Chosakuken Kyōgikai, 1951–.

VI-14. *Shokuinroku.* Tokyo: Ōkurashō Insatsukyoku, 1886–.

VI-15. *Kenkyūsha kenkyū kadai sōran: Jinbun shakai kagaku hen.* Tokyo: Nihon Gakujutsu Shinkōkai, 1979–.

VI-16. *Daijinmei jiten.* Tokyo: Heibonsha, 1953–55. 10v. An earlier edition of this, called *Shinsen daijinmei jiten,* was published between 1937 and 1941, was reprinted with minor changes as *Nihon jinmei daijiten* in 1979 in 7 volumes.

VI-17. Nichigai Asoshieitsu. *Namae kara hiku jinmei jiten.* Tokyo: Nichigai Asoshieitsu, 1988. 6, 1,104p.

VI-18. Ōue Shirō, comp. *Meiji kakocho: Bukko jinmei jiten shinteiban,* rev. ed. Tokyo: Tōkyō Bijutsu, 1971. 167, 1,264p.

VI-19. Inamura Tetsugen, et al. *Taishō kakochō: Bukko jinmei jiten.* Tokyo: Tōkyō Bijutsu, 1973. 466p.

VI-20. *Shōwa bukko jinmeiroku 1926–79.* Tokyo: Nichigai Asoshieitsu, 1983. 747p.

VI-21. *Gendai bukkosha jiten 1980–82.* Tokyo: Nichigai Asoshieitsu, 1983, 417p.

VI-22. *Japan Who Was Who: Bukkosha jiten 1983–87.* Tokyo: Nichigai Asoshieitsu, 1988. 780p.

VI-23. *Iwanami Seiyō jinmei jiten*, new and enl. ed. Tokyo: Iwanami Shoten, 1981. 1,962, 282p.

VI-24. Takeuchi Hiroshi. *Rainichi Seiyō jinmei jiten*. Tokyo: Nichigai Asoshieitsu, 1983. 21, 646p.

VI-25. *Jinbutsu refarensu jiten*. Tokyo: Nichigai Asoshieitsu, 1983. 4v. in 7.

VI-26. Nihon Rekishi Gakkai. *Jinbutsu sōsho*. Tokyo: Yoshikawa Kōbunkan, 1958–.

VI-27. Ōta Akira. *Seishi kakei daijiten*. Tokyo: Seishi Kakei Daijiten Kankōkai, 1934–36. 3v.

VI-28. Hioki Shōichi. *Nihon keifu sōran*. Tokyo: Kaizōsha, 1936. 36, 984p.

VI-29. Maruyama Kōichi. *Keizu bunken shiryō sōran,* rev. and enl. ed. Tokyo: Ryokuin Shobō, 1992. 916p.

VI-30. Kondō Yasutarō. *Keizu kenkyū no kiso chishiki: Kakei ni miru Nihon no rekishi*. Tokyo: Kondō Shuppansha, 1989–90. 4v.

VI-31. Hōsei Daigaku. Bungakubu. Shigaku Kenkyūshitsu. *Nihon jinbutsu bunken mokuroku*. Tokyo: Heibonsha, 1974. 4, 1,199p.

VI-32. Fukai Hitoshi. *Jinbutsu shoshi sakuin*. Tokyo: Nichigai Asoshieitsu, 1979. xxxiv, 400p.

VI-33. Kokuritsu Kokkai Toshokan. *Jinbutsu bunken sakuin*. Tokyo: Kokuritsu Kokkai Toshokan, 1967–72. 3v.

VI-34. *Nenkan jinbutsu bunken mokuroku*. Tokyo: Nichigai Asoshieitsu, 1980–.

VI-35. *Denki, hyōden zenjōhō 45/89: Nihon Tōyō hen*. Tokyo: Nichigai Asoshieitsu, 1991. 2v.

VI-36. Nichigai Asoshieitsu. *Jinbutsu shoshi taikei*. Tokyo: Nichigai Asoshieitsu, 1982–.

Chapter Seven
Dictionaries and Encyclopedias

While conducting a bibliographic search, it is not uncommon to come across titles of books you cannot read or words you do not understand. You might have to spend more time on those problems than on your original search. Knowing which dictionary to use for what purpose could eventually save you a tremendous amount of time and frustration. Thus, here we will discuss various types of dictionaries.

When you first started to study Japanese, you probably used Nelson's *The Modern Reader's Japanese-English Character Dictionary* and the Japan Foundation's *Basic Japanese-English Dictionary*. Both of them are very good dictionaries, but they contain limited vocabularies and characters, and after a while you must move on to other dictionaries. There are two types of word dictionaries in Japanese. One type, indexed by Chinese characters, is called *Kan-Wa jiten*; the other, arranged by Japanese syllabary, is called *Kokugo jiten*.

1. *KAN-WA JITEN*

Problem VII-1. How do you read 灵 in 死灵 ? It appears in the script of a Kabuki play.
Problem VII-2. How do you read 晩酌 ? What is its meaning and correct usage?

When you want to find the readings and meanings of Chinese characters, use *Kan-Wa jiten* 漢和辞典, Chinese-Japanese dictionaries. Sometimes you can guess the readings, and sometimes you can't. For example, how would you read 鰯, "fish" radical plus "weak"? Weak fish? What kind of fish is 魞 ? The first *kanji* is read *iwashi*, "sardine," and the second one is read *eri*, which is not a fish but a fish trap. At least in this case it has something to do with fish, and the character makes sense in a way, because it is written "fish enters." But how about 魯, "fish" plus "sun"? This character is read *ro*, and means "stupid," or the name of ancient Chinese state, which has nothing to do with fish.

Usually dictionaries are compiled and arranged in such a way that they are not meant to be read. Some are arranged easily, but some are more difficult to use. It is important, therefore, to read the *hanrei* 凡例 , "explanatory notes," carefully. You should also make it a habit to use more than one dictionary or encyclopedia when possible.

When you want to find out the readings and meanings of Chinese characters, you can use any *Kan-Wa jiten*, including *Nelson's*. Unlike *Nelson's*, which is arranged by radicals only, regular *Kan-Wa jiten* are equipped with two other convenient and important access methods in addition to an index by radicals: an *on* (sound)-reading index and *kun* (Japanese reading of Chinese characters)-reading index. Of all the *Kan-Wa jiten*, you should be familiar with Morohashi's *Dai Kan-Wa jiten* 大漢和辞典 (VII-1). It is so authoritative that there is a Chinese translation, *Chung-wen ta tzu-tien* 中文大辞典 published in Taiwan. *Dai Kan-Wa jiten*, often referred to as *Morohashi* to show respect for the main compiler, is the most extensive and authoritative dictionary of Chinese characters. It took thirty-five years and numerous people to complete. About 50,000 characters and over 500,000 words appear in this book, which constitutes Morohashi's life work. Not only orthodox Chinese characters, but also abbreviated or commonly used simplified forms, as well as *kokuji* (characters composed in Japan), are included. For each character the writing variations of that character, the Chinese and Japanese pronunciations and definitions, and compounds starting with that character are given. Idioms and phrases, place-names, titles of books and plays, Buddhist terms, *nengō*, and personal names are listed as entries. Although the coverage of Chinese personal names is broad, Japanese names are limited to those of Chinese classical scholars. This *Dai Kan-Wa jiten* is arranged by radical, and the indexes are arranged by stroke count, four corners, and *on* 音 and *kun* 訓 readings. An appendix lists the simplified characters of mainland China.

In using this work, students must be aware that all entries appear under the most orthodox, unsimplified form of the *kanji*. Compounds are alphabetized in あいうえお order, but by classical Japanese spellings. The greater part of the definitions will be in

Sample page of Dai Kan-Wa jiten

classical Japanese, or slightly modified *kanbun*. In addition, the sheer comprehensiveness of the work makes it quite tedious to use and impractical for run-of-the-mill questions.

Dai Kan-Wa jiten is arranged by old-style characters (*kyū kanji*), and the reading of *kanji* is given in the old-style reading. It thus became increasingly difficult for younger generations who are used to new-style characters (*shin kanji*) and new *kanazukai* to consult this dictionary. This difficulty was recognized by the compilers, and the vocabulary and phrase index now features both styles. Although *Dai Kan-Wa jiten: Goi sakuin* 大漢和辞典：語彙索引 (VII-2) was prepared at the time the revised edition was published, it can also be used with the earlier editions.

Kō Kan-Wa jiten 広漢和辞典 (VII-3) is a modernized and simplified version of the monumental *Dai Kan-Wa jiten*. The authors spent twenty years in compiling this updated, easy-to-use dictionary, which is designed to meet the current needs of scholars and the general public. They selected 20,000 root Chinese characters out of the 50,000 in *Dai Kan-Wa jiten*, and 120,000 compounds out of the 500,000 in *Dai Kan-Wa jiten* for this four-volume dictionary. The entries are under the new form of the characters when applicable, and the old forms are listed directly under the new forms, as opposed to *Dai Kan-Wa jiten* where entries are by the old form of the character. Chinese pronunciation in *pinyin* romanization, difficult readings, and antonyms are some of the new features of this wonderful dictionary. A particular effort was made to include simplified Chinese characters, Japanese figures appearing in classics, Japanese compounds, and Japanese words written with Chinese characters. The index volume includes a new feature: an index for compound words in Japanese syllabary order.

Dai Kangorin 大漢語林 (VII-4) was compiled to meet the needs of the general public at home and office. This extensive one-volume desk dictionary contains 13,938 characters, including variant forms and Japanese characters. Entries are under the new-style character, and then the old-style character. Traditionally, 214 radicals were used, but for ease of use, some radicals were changed. All the Japan Industrial Standard (JIS) characters are included. When the current reading is different from the traditional reading, it also appears. *Dai Kangorin goi sōran* 大漢語林 語彙総覧 (VII-5) is arranged in Japanese syllabary order and allows you to go directly to

Sample page of Kō Kan-Wa jiten

the correct page if you know the reading. If you don't know how to read the compound, check the reading list for the first character. Regardless, you can save time by consulting this dictionary.

Daijiten 大字典 (VII-6) compiled by Ueda Kazutoshi 上田万年, sometimes includes Chinese characters that are not found even in Morohashi's *Dai Kan-Wa jiten*. It is particularly strong in *kokuji* 国字, characters made in Japan, and various forms of *ryakuji* 略字, simplified characters. This dictionary was reprinted in the United States during World War II because it contains numerous characters for its size. After seventy-five years this dictionary was extensively revised and renamed *Shin Daijiten* 新大字典 (VII-7). The new edition includes 21,094 characters, as opposed to the 14,924 of the original edition, and 110,000 compounds. Old-style characters are still used as the form of the entry, but simplified and popularized characters are also included. There is an easy-to-use radical index, an *on-kun* index, and a stroke-count index.

Nankun jiten 難訓辞典 (VII-8) by Nakayama Yasumasa is a dictionary of words that comprise Chinese characters with special and difficult readings. The first part of the dictionary includes readings and definitions of common nouns and the second part includes proper nouns such as family names and geographical names. It is arranged according to the stroke count of Chinese characters and contains no index. An appendix lists words starting with numbers.

Longer Chinese classical phrases that tend not to be in regular *Kan-Wa jiten* have to be looked up using *koji jukugo jiten* 故事熟語辞典, dictionaries of fables and phrases.

Another *kanji* dictionary for the native speaker of English needs special mention here. It is *Kan-Ei jukugo ribaasu jiten* 漢英熟語リバース字典 (VII-9) (Japanese character dictionary with compound lookup via any *kanji*). This is truly unique and one of the most useful trilingual dictionaries of Chinese characters to be compiled for non-native speakers of Japanese. It has been arranged to make it as easy as possible to look up the readings and meanings of Japanese words written in Chinese characters. Nearly 6,000 characters and 1,000 variants are included. In all, it contains nearly 47,000 compounds that were selected from various books and articles, and from other dictionaries. It enables the user to search under any character whether it is the first, the second, the third, or even the last of the components. Characters are arranged under easy-to-check radicals. *Shin Kan-Ei*

3i5.4

```
                              3i5.6/918
                                    Ō go; the first yu(ku) go
                 subjugate the barbarians      i(nasu) let go; parry (an
    征伐 seibatsu subjugate, conquer, punish,   attack in sumo)
         exterminate              往[徃]
    征衣 seii military uniform; traveling  ─────── 1st ───────
         clothes                  3往々 ōō sometimes, occasionally, often
  8 征服 seifuku conquer, subjugate; master   4往日 ōjitsu ancient times
    征服者 seifukusha conqueror      5往生 ōjō die (and be reborn in paradise);
    征服欲 seifukuyoku desire for conquest     give in; be at one's wit's end
  9 征途 seito military expedition; journey   往生際悪 ōjōgiwa (ga) waru(i) accept
 10 征討 seitō subjugation, pacification       defeat with bad grace
 13 征戦 seisen military expedition   往古 ōko ancient times
  ─────── 2nd ───────            6往年 ōnen in years gone by
  5 出征 shussei depart for the front, go to  7往来 ōrai coming and going, traffic; road,
         war                          street; fluc
    外征 gaisei foreign expedition/campaign   往来止 ōraido(me) Road Closed
  8 長征 chōsei long march         8往事 ōji the past
 12 遠征 ensei (military) expedition, campaign;  往往 ōō sometimes, occasionally, often
         tour (by a team)         9往信 ōshin letter/message requesting a
    遠征隊 enseitai expeditionary forces,      reply
         invaders; visiting team  10往時 ōji ancient times
 16 親征 shinsei military expedition led by the  往航 ōkō outward voyage
         emperor                   11往訪 ōhō visit, call on
                                 12往復 ōfuku going and returning, round trip;
 3i5.4                               correspondence; association
       SO go                       往復切符 ōfuku kippu round trip ticket
    阻                              往復葉書 ōfuku hagaki return postcard
    低→低    2a5.15                 往診 ōshin doctor's visit, house call
                                 13往路 ōro outward journey
 3i5.5/1475                      15往還 ōkan coming and going, traffic; road
                                  ─────── 2nd ───────
    径[徑逕]  KEI path; diameter  3大往生 daiōjō a peaceful death
  ─────── 1st ───────            5古往今来 koō-konrai in all ages, since
  6 径行 keikō go right ahead           antiquity
  9 径庭 keitei great difference    右往左往 uō-saō go hither and thither
 13 径路 keiro course, route, process   立往生 ta(chi)ōjō be at a standstill, be
  ─────── 2nd ───────                 stalled/stranded; stand speechless
  3 口径 kōkei caliber, bore, aperture     (without a rejoinder)
    小径 shōkei lane, path         8往往 ōō sometimes, occasionally, often
    山径 sankei mountain path      9独往 dokuō going one's own way
  4 内径 naikei inside diameter   10既往 kiō the past
  5 半径 hankei radius              既往症 kiōshō previous illness, medical
    外径 gaikei outside diameter       history
  8 直径 chokkei diameter            既往歴 kiōreki patient's medical history
 11 捷径 shōkei short cut, shorter way  ─────── 3rd ───────
  ─────── 3rd ───────           12極楽往生 gokuraku ōjō a peaceful death
  3 大口径 daikōkei large-caliber    無理往生 muri-ōjō forced compliance
  8 直情径行 chokujō keikō straightforward,  ─────── 4th ───────
         impulsive               5右往左往 uō-saō go hither and thither
  ─────── 4th ───────            ─────── 6 ───────
  6 行動半径 kōdō hankei radius of action,
         range                 3i6.1/667
                                    RITSU, RICHI law, regulation; rhythm
                                律
```

Sample page of Kan-Ei jukugo ribaasu jiten

jiten 新漢英字典, *New Japanese-English Character Dictionary* by Jack Halpern (Tokyo: Kenkyūsha, 1990; 2,224 p.) is another convenient Chinese character dictionary for English, or nonnative speakers of Japanese.

Returning to problem VII-1, how to read 灵 in 死灵, the character does not appear in either *Dai Kan-Wa jiten* or *Kō Kan-Wa jiten*. If you are persistent, however, and go to *Daijiten*, you will find it listed as a simplified form of 靈. You can confirm its reading in that compound by checking under 死, which you will find under *shiryō* in all three dictionaries.

While we are considering *Kan-Wa jiten*, we can check 晩酌 (problem VII-2). 晩 incorporates the "sun" radical, which has four strokes. If you want to check by the radical, you must go to the radical index. Besides the radical, which is *hen* 篇, you count the strokes for *tsukuri* 旁 or "remainder." In this case, 免 has eight strokes. Under the "sun" radical, you find 晩, whose reading is *ban*, meaning "evening," or "late." If the dictionary you are using is large enough, you will find this compound listed, and you can find both reading and meaning at the same time. If it is a small dictionary, it might not be listed. In that case, you start the same procedure with the second character in the compound, which is 酌. The radical for 酌 is 酉, and it contains seven strokes. Fortunately, the radical index under 七画, seven strokes, shows 酉. *Tsukuri* consists of three strokes, and you find 酌. The reading is *shaku*, "ladle, scoop up." If you check the larger *Kan-Wa jiten*, you will learn the meaning of the compound. If you are checking in a smaller one, you might have to go to one of the *kokugo jiten*, which has a larger number of definitions.

Comparing definitions for the same word, *banshaku*, in different dictionaries, we find the following:

Dictionary	Definition	Sample Sentence
Dai Kan-Wa jiten	Yūgata ni nomu sake. Nezake.	Yes (in Chinese)
Kō Kan-Wa jiten	Yūgata ni nomu sake. Ban no shokuji no toki ni sake o nomu koto.	Yes
Daijiten	Ban no shokuji ni sake o nomu	No
Nihon kokugo daijiten	Yūhan no toki ni sake o nomu koto. Mata sono sake.	Yes
Gakken kokugo daijiten	(Katei de) Yūhan no toki sake o nomu koto. Mata sono sake.	Yes

Kōjien	Ban no shokuji no toki ni sake o nomu koto. Mata sono sake.	No
Nihongo daijiten	Yūshoku no toki ni sake o nomu koto. Mata sono sake. Evening drink.	No
Daijirin	(Katei de) Ban no shokuji no toki sake o nomu koto. Mata sono sake.	No
Gensen	Yūhan no toki ni sake o nomu koto. Mata sono sake.	Yes
Kenkyūsha Wa-Ei daijiten	An evening drink.	Yes

Not even all these major dictionaries are successful individually or collectively in defining the core meaning or the nuance of *banshaku*, which the Japanese can unmistakably discriminate. *Banshaku [o suru]* implies originally that the head of a household (husband) drinks *sake* habitually, in the evening, alone, at home, and at or before supper, for relaxation. We hope, however, this comparison of several similar dictionaries will show that it is not sufficient to consult one dictionary. *Kan-Wa jiten* include simpler explanations for this particular word. Close examination of sample sentences in *Kan-Wa jiten* and *kokugo jiten* will reveal a slight difference between these two types of language dictionaries. It is better to check words, particularly those closely related to Japanese culture, in *kokugo jiten*, even if you have to find out the readings of these words in *Kan-Wa jiten*.

2. KOKUGO JITEN

You can use any *kokugo jiten* 国語辞典, such as *Nihon kokugo daijiten* 日本国語大辞典, *Daijirin* 大辞林, *Gensen = Kokugo daijiten* 言泉=国語大辞典, *Nihongo daijiten* 日本語大辞典, and *Kōjien* 広辞苑, to look up the meanings of Japanese words. Of these dictionaries, *Nihongo daijiten* (VII-10) is probably the easiest and most convenient one for the readers of this textbook. It is an encyclopedic, modern Japanese language dictionary that aims to give a total picture of the language. It contains 175,000 words, terms, and phrases, names that are encountered and used daily, and sample sentences that employ the words. Explanations are simple and clear. This dictionary has many unique features such as 8,800 old sayings and idiomatic phrases and Chinese characters in large print to facilitate

あいちよ——あいつち

あいちょう-しゅうかん【愛鳥週間】【名】 アイテウシウカン〔愛鳥週間〕 野鳥など、鳥を愛護する週間。毎年五月一〇日からの一週間。バードウィーク。《季・夏》 発音 アイチョーシューカン 標ア② 奈ア②

あいち-ようすい【愛知用水】 アイチヨースイ 木曾川から濃尾平野東部と知多半島に引いた農工業用水。昭和三六年完成。幹線水路の延長一一二キロメートル。支線水路の延長一三五キロメートル。 発音 アイチヨースイ 標ア③ 奈ア③

あい-ちよく【愛陟】【名】 好んで歩くこと。〔庭園などを好んで散歩すること。〕 *剣菴十種〈栗本鋤雲〉暁窓追録「昕夕愛陟の園池を棄廃するは、殆んど不平愁苦の情無き不〻能べし」

あい-ちん【名】「あいちゃん」に同じ。〔隠語輯覧〕

あい-つ【彼奴】【代名】(「あやつ」の変化したもの。遠慮なく言ったりする場合の人物をののしったり、または乱暴な話し方で事物などを指示し、または聞き手両者から離れた人、事物などを指し示す(遠称)。話し手、聞き手両者から離れた人、事物などを指し示す(遠称)。比興なものと思へども」 *虎明本狂言・鏡男「わらわがかほを、あいつにまぶらせうと思ふて、みようよ」 ＊四河入海一五・三「心にはあいつといふな」 ＊口葡辞書「Aitçu（アイツ）、〈訳〉あの男。軽蔑や卑下を伴って言う」 ＊洒落本・辰巳之園「西村の船頭か。あいつも見わすれたそふな」 ●風

ば」 ＊漢書-杜欽伝「好憎之心生、則愛寵偏於一人」

あい-つう【哀痛】【名】 かなしみいたむこと。ひどくかなしむこと。 ＊文明本節用集「哀痛 アイツウ」 ＊思出の記〈徳富蘆花〉巻外・六「昔し吾眼下に見た魯鈍者〈略〉の下に立つ運命に会へる者少なからざるを見て哀痛に不堪（たえず）候」 ＊長塚節歌集〈長塚節〉明治三六年「哀痛悲懺禁することを能はず」 ＊荀子-礼論「哀痛未レ尽、思慕未レ忘」 発音 アイツー 標ア② 古辞書 文明

あい-つう・する あひつ…【相通】(「あい」は接頭語) 一 〘自サ変〙因 あひつう・ず〘自サ変〙互いに通い合う。わかりあうものなれば、彼是（ひし）相通（アヒツウ）ずると、大変な間違になる」 二〘他サ変〙因 あひつう・ず〘他サ変〙 ㈠同じ金で代表さして、永日小品〈夏目漱石〉金「同じ金で代表さして、彼是（ひし）相通（アヒツウ）ずると、大変な間違になる」 ㈡〘他サ変〙互いに連絡をとる。通い合うようにする。小説神髄〈坪内逍遙〉下・脚色の法則「脈絡通徹（みゃくらくつうてつ）とは篇中の事物巨細となく互に脈絡を相通（アイツウ）じて相隔離せざることをいふなり」 発音 アイツーズル 標ア⑦ 古辞書 文明

った」 ＊土〈長塚節〉一一「此細であるとはいひながら、相尋（アヒツイ）で彼等の耳に聞えるので」

エラフツク【会津絵蝋燭】【名】

recognition by foreigners. Particularly useful are its indexes to over 8,000 characters and the *on* and *kun* readings for each character. These enable the user to go directly to the index when he does not know the pronunciation of a character, rather than first consulting a Chinese character dictionary for pronunciation and then going to the right entry word. Another helpful feature is the inclusion of an English equivalent under the appropriate entry word. Under each entry, the Chinese character is given along with its meaning or, for foreign words, original spelling. In the case of ordinary Japanese words, the current and most common meaning is given first, with examples of its usage. Entries also include counters, which are often problems for nonnative speakers. Yet another characteristic of this dictionary is the abundant use of visual aids. It functions as an encyclopedia for daily use, a Japanese-English and Chinese character dictionary, a dictionary of idioms, phrases, synonyms, and loanwords, as well as an excellent Japanese-language dictionary.

The most important *kokugo jiten* is *Nihon kokugo daijiten* (VII-11). This encyclopedic dictionary of Japanese language was created to be the "OED of Japan," and its compilers accomplished that goal. Nearly 500,000 words are collected from earlier Japanese language dictionaries, especially *Dai Nihon kokugo jiten* compiled by Ueda Kazutoshi and Matsui Kanji (Tokyo: Fuzanbō, 1949; 5v.), and numerous other sources for all the periods. The dictionary contains not only words from all periods that are normally found in Japanese language dictionaries, but also geographical and personal names, technical terms, loan words, dialects, slang terms, titles of books and plays, proverbs, and idioms. The history of each Japanese word is included. Roughly two million examples collected from over 10,000 various sources of all the periods are included. It is arranged in Japanese syllabary order.

A new, long-awaited dictionary is the *gyakubiki jiten,* or reverse-word order dictionary. *Gyakubiki jukugorin* 逆引き熟語林 and *Gyakubiki Kōjien* 逆引き広辞苑 are two examples. The former includes 142,000 Chinese compounds and Japanese words written in Chinese but read in Japanese. The latter has 200,000 entries and was carefully prepared; the inclusion of lists of 6,000 important word endings is a nice feature. Of the two, *Gyakubiki Kōjien* is the more detailed dictionary; *Gyakubiki jukugorin* is easier to use.

Languages change over time, and even the most up-to-date dictionary will become outdated sooner or later. Since larger dictionaries go through major revisions only every twenty or so years, it is important to check supplementary dictionaries for new words and specialized terminology found in recent publications. There are numerous dictionaries for general and specific terms, and you should familiarize yourself with those in your field in order to more efficiently conduct your research.

Kadokawa kogo daijiten 角川古語大辞典 (VII-12) is projected to appear in four volumes and will be the most extensive and authoritative dictionary of archaic words. It will contain 80,000 words, including literary words, poetic terms, words used in proverbs, slang terms, the vocabulary of red-light districts, and more, collected from 4,000 sources. It has explanations of the basic meanings of words and includes many words that are still in use. For each definition an example is included. Special attention was paid to explain the differences among synonyms or related words, with an explanation of the changes in the meanings of words, by periods. It is full of unique illustrations to aid the user's understanding.

Iwanami kogo jiten 岩波古語辞典 (VII-13) is an authoritative and convenient dictionary containing 43,000 words found in pre-1730 historical and literary texts. It also has convenient appendixes. For a specific period, use dictionaries such as *Edogo daijiten* 江戸語大辞典 (VII-14), which contains 30,000 Edo-period words of the commoner's class, or *Jidaibetsu kokugo daijiten* 時代別国語大辞典.

Since extensive dictionaries and encyclopedias are not revised often, newly created words and new technical terms should be looked up in more current reference works. For new words and words on current topics turn to the following three dictionaries. *Gendai yōgo no kiso chishiki* 現代用語の基礎知識 (VII-15) has been published annually since 1948, and essays explaining words in each subject area are written by specialists in each field. *Jōhō chishiki imidas* 情報知識イミダス (VII-16) and *Asahi Shinbun gendai yōgo Chiezo* 朝日現代用語 知恵蔵 (VII-17) are new. All three are good and are equipped with good indexes and with similar arrangements and information. You can also use any *shingo jiten* 新語辞典, the neologism, or dictionary of newly coined words, as long as its date of publication is reasonably recent.

For loanwords, the standard dictionary is *Kadokawa gairaigo jiten* 角川外来語辞典 by Arakawa Sōbei あらかわそおべえ (VII-18). The second edition includes over 27,000 loanwords selected from varieties of sources and arranged in Japanese syllabary order. Each entry is in *katakana*, followed by the language identification number, original word, language of origin, linguistic notes, and the meaning. An enlarged section containing revisions has been added (pp. 1,534-1,643). The strength of this dictionary is its abundance of examples with sources. *Kihon gairaigo jiten* 基本外来語辞典 is a smaller dictionary of basic loanwords, excluding personal and place-names, and it concentrates more on recent words.

Japanese has many dialects, and students in Japanese studies are destined to come across ones they don't know sooner or later. In such cases, turn to a dialect dictionary, such as *Nihon hōgen daijiten* 日本方言大辞典 (VII-19), which is the most extensive work compiled by a recognized authority on dialects. Approximately 40,000 words in Japanese dialects are arranged in Japanese syllabary order. The part of speech is recorded if the word is not a noun, followed by the meaning of the word, the locality where it is used, and examples. It includes an introductory essay on Japanese dialects. *Gendai Nihongo hōgen daijiten* 現代日本語方言大辞典 is not a dictionary to consult if you don't know the meaning of a dialect you heard. This is an enormous collection of the dialects currently in use in the seventy-two regions of Japan, and it includes basic vocabulary.

The Japanese language often changes accent from dialect to dialect. *Nihongo hatsuon akusento jiten* 日本語発音アクセント辞典 (VII-20) can be used to check the intonation pattern of approximately 70,000 Japanese words. The main part of the dictionary is an alphabetical listing of words with the accent marked for a standard Tokyo pronunciation, followed by the intonation pattern for the regional dialects in Kyoto and Kagoshima. Unless you are interested in Japanese phonology, however, you can bypass this dictionary.

Slang is also another difficult category in the Japanese language. *Ingo jiten* 隠語辞典 (VII-21), the dictionary of slang or "secret language" in Japan, includes approximately 17,000 words used by special occupational or social groups, such as gangsters and ex-convicts.

Is there anything like *Roget's Thesaurus*? *Kadokawa ruigo shinjiten* 角川類語新辞典 (VII-22) by Ōno Susumu and Hamanishi Masando, the first extensive thesaurus of the Japanese language, includes 60,000 words, phrases, idioms, and proverbs that are primarily modern in origin. These words are categorized and arranged systematically by a decimal system into 1,000 groups. There are two

DICTIONARIES AND ENCYCLOPEDIAS

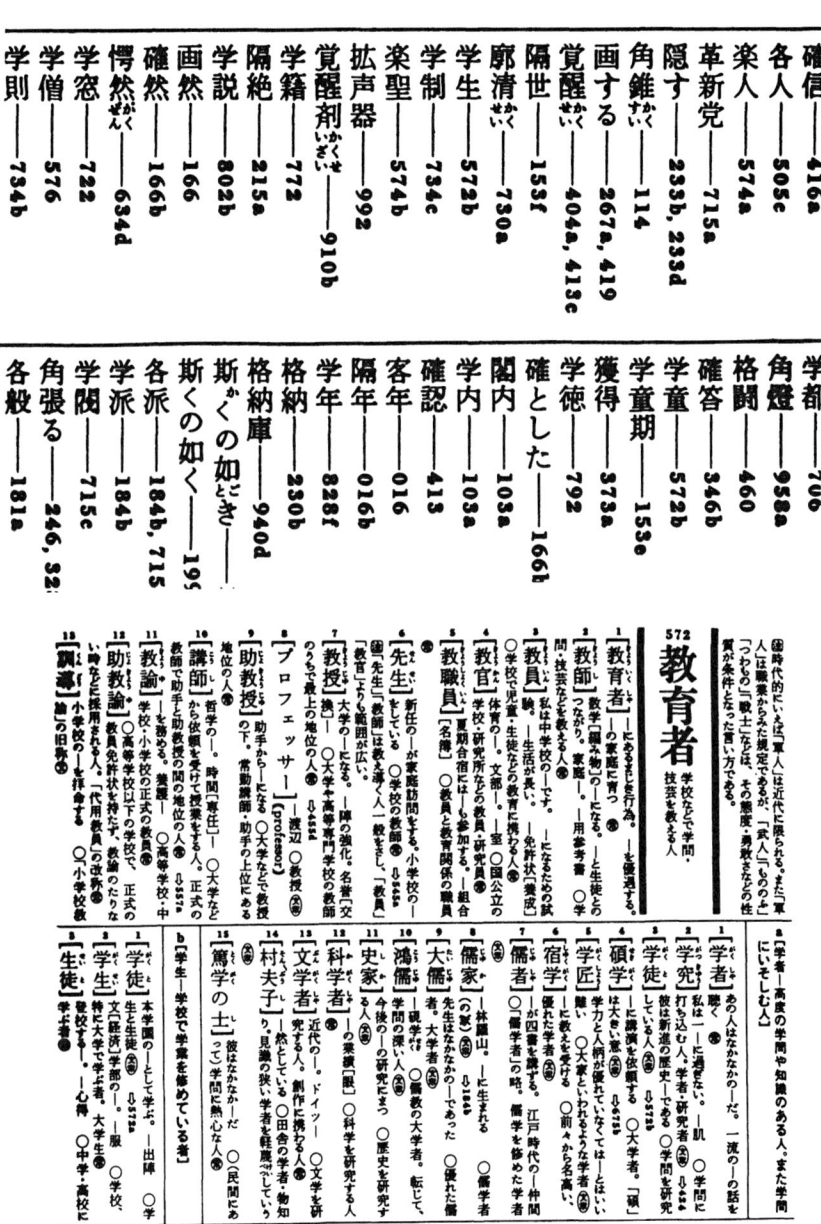

Sample page of Kadokawa ruigo shinjiten

せ

せいせい 息を、短く、強く、繰り返し して。息遣いが荒く。
【せいせい（息を）弾ませる】〈《危ねい！ 往来の真ン中を彷徨してやがって……》と せいせい息を逸ませながら立止って怒鳴り つけたのは、目の怕い車夫であった。(平 凡十九・二葉亭四迷)〉

ぜいぜい 息を、短く、激しく、繰り返し 出して。息遣いが、激しく荒く。
【ぜいぜい呼吸をする】〈メロスは馬のや うに大きな胴震ひを一つして、すぐにまた 先を急いだ。(略)ぜいぜい荒い呼吸を しながら峠をのぼり、のぼり切って、ほつ とした時、突然、目の前に一隊の山賊が躍 り出た。(走れメロス・太宰治)〉

せいせいと さっぱりと。快く。
【（心）（気）が】せいせいとす。(する)】〈シテやいやい磁石。アドへ何ぢや。シテへ この太刀を見すれば何とある。アドへ心が 晴々とする。(磁石・狂言三百番集) 〈ヘ(シテ)へ まく まく する。(磁石・狂言三百番集)〉〈(シテ)へ此の 太刀をかうふり上げた所は何と有るぞ。 (アド)夫を呑まう呑まうとおもうて気が晴 々とする。(同・鷺狂言)〉〈今汝が太刀を見 れば、清々として呑みたいほどに、切先 から只一呑みにせうぞ。(同・続狂言記五、 七)〉

せいせい ぜいぜい ぜえぜえ
同じ系列と考えられる。「せいせい と」は、「清々と・晴々と」などで、 漢語起源か。

Sample page of Giseigo gitaigo kan'yōku jiten

major ways of consulting this thesaurus. If you have a certain word in mind, go directly to the index arranged in Japanese syllabary order at the end of the volume. For example, if you know the word *gakusei* 学生 ("high-school students") and are looking for a synonym, the index guides you to 572b, under the word for "profession," subcategory "educator," then "students" (*gakusei*). Under *gakusei*, eighteen words are listed. Two words, *seito* 生徒 and *kōkōsei* 高校生 might fit your purpose. A second way to use the book is to browse to find which words are equivalent to a particular English word. For example, to find the equivalent of the English "you," turn to the index printed on the end papers of the book. Because this word is related to "people," go to *jinji* 人事, or "human affairs." When you find *jinbutsu* 人物, "people," look for the suitable section. Category 50 is *ninshō*, "personal pronouns." Turn to 5, *jinbutsu*, and look at the detailed index there. Under *ninshō* 人称, you find that word 502 on page 448 is *taishō* 対称, which is the grammatical term for the second-person pronoun, "you." *Taishō* is divided into three sections. The first one lists nineteen different words that mean "you." The second section lists second-person pronouns where the person is younger than or inferior to you. The last section is for the plural "you." Generally speaking, the most common word is given first, and examples of usage along with detailed meaning, type of word, (literary, colloquial, old-fashioned, common, etc.), and gender of the user, when applicable, are given.

One unique characteristic of the Japanese language is the frequent occurrence and richness of onomatopoeias such as *harahara*, *chirachira*, *berabera*, and *perapera*. Three or four good dictionaries cover examples collected from classical and modern works, but one fairly extensive one is *Giseigo gitaigo kan'yōku jiten* 擬声語擬態語慣用句辞典 (VII-23) by Shiraishi Daiji.

Although a dictionary like *Nihon kokugo daijiten* includes etymology, *Nihongo gogen jiten* 国語語源辞典 (VII-24) is an example of an etymological dictionary of the Japanese language. The etymology of the Japanese language is very difficult and gives rise to various theories and interpretations, and therefore you should not rely on just one etymological dictionary.

Japanese often use *koji jukugo*, which are strings of Chinese characters of fables and phrases often based on Chinese historical events and old sayings. Another type of word dictionary is the *kotowaza jiten,* dictionaries of proverbs and old sayings. *Koji zokushin kotowaza daijiten* 故事俗信ことわざ大辞典 (VII-25) and *Seigorin: Koji kotowaza kan'yōku* 成語林 (VII-26) can be used for both purposes. *Seigorin* is particularly good for the reader because it includes how and how not to use the words. *Koji zokushin kotowaza daijiten* includes much more than what the title indicates. It also includes word games and traditional poetry. The strongest point of this extensive dictionary is its extensive word index, which enables the user to find almost anything in the dictionary. For Chinese fables and phrases, *Koji seigo meigen daijiten* 故事成語名言大辞典 is also an excellent dictionary.

Many other kinds of dictionaries also exist in Japan, and the knowledge of unique dictionaries in your own field will help you effectively search for information on words. Familiarize yourself with these dictionaries by consulting *Nihon no sankō tosho* (V-3) and other reference works. You could then easily find, for example, the different readings and meanings of the word 地方 in a dictionary of historical terms.

Quiz VII-1. I am looking for information on *ashidaka no sei* 足高の制, a term used during the Edo period. I am not sure if the reading is correct.

3. ENCYCLOPEDIAS

Problem VII-3. I would like to find out about *mogi* 裳著, a word appearing in *Genji monogatari*. I would like to know the origin and the history of the word and also how the word appeared in other sources.

When you need fairly detailed information on something, go to general encyclopedias rather than regular dictionaries. Among many encyclopedias, *Sekai daihyakka jiten* 新世界大百科事典 (VII-27) is probably the most common. Printed in large type, entry words number approximately 90,000, while the index includes 400,000 words. There were 7,000 authors, and it includes nearly 20,000 illustrations (10,000 in black and white; 8,500 in color). When you refer to it, or to any encyclopedia, remember to turn to the index volume first, even when the arrangement of the set is in Japanese syllabary order.

Koji ruien 古事類苑 (VII-28) is the last of the traditional Chinese-style encyclopedias, *lei-shu* 類書. First published between 1896 and 1914, it is a collection of primary source materials selected from books published before 1868. Intended to preserve traditional Japanese culture, it covers all the phases of life in premodern Japan. Classified by subject into thirty sections, it is indispensable for historical and literary studies and is particularly useful as a reference work for users with an advanced knowledge of classical Japanese.

You can solve problem VII-3 using *Koji ruien*. Go to the index volume and find the word *mogi*. Here you will find the word written in a different way in *Reishiki-bu* [Section on Ceremonies and Rites] 1, p. 601. When you turn to this page, you will find information on the ceremony, alternate names, when the ceremony was performed, and where the word appeared in various classical texts. You will notice there is a big difference between the entry under *mogi* in *Koji ruien* and the entry in the modern encyclopedia. Any encyclopedia would summarize the information about *mogi*, but only *Koji ruien* gives passages where the word appears. This is one of the main reasons why *Koji ruien*, an old-fashioned encyclopedia, is still indispensable.

Another encyclopedia that needs to be mentioned here is the most comprehensive English-language work, the *Kodansha Encyclopedia of Japan* (VII-29). It boasts 9,417 entries and covers subjects in the humanities, social sciences, and natural sciences, as well as all aspects of Japanese life. The length of the entries differs by the importance of the topic. Some articles are signed and contain bibliographies at the end, but they are lacking in many entries where the user might need a study guide or bibliography. English was chosen for most of the entry words, but some are entered in Japanese in their romanized form. The encyclopedia is arranged in alphabetical order and is illustrated with black-and-white illustrations. Volume 9, the index volume, provides access to 50,000 words. Some entries in the index include Japanese writings. Despite the noticeable shortage of bibliographies in many articles, this is still an indispensable work on Japan and its culture and provides a starting point for many English-speaking students and researchers.

There seems to be at least one subject encyclopedia or encyclopedic dictionary in almost every field of study. *Engeki hyakka daijiten* is one such encyclopedia. When you cannot locate a suitable dictionary or subject encyclopedia in your own field, check guides to reference tools such as *Nihon no sankō tosho: Kaisetsu sōran* or

水注子

〔延喜式三十四　神事并年料供御〕
居。水．硯．案　尺。高四二尺。長尺広功二二二人人尺中短五功功寸。二三厚人人八。牛分。

〔書言字考節用集七〕附　水注子。

〔頭書増補訓蒙図彙器用十一〕注子。水注子は水さし、湯盞湯釜に、湯のあつきとき、水をうめる具なり、

此亦櫃雪時須也。

注子

〔事物紀原什物器用〕注子
事始曰、唐元和初、酌酒用樽杓、雖十數人、一樽一杓、挹酒了無遺滴、無幾改用注子、難起自元和時、而顧失其所造之人、

〔和漢茶誌二〕注子　水壺也、俗名注子云、金胡銅、金紫銅胡銅之屬今水檣、
古者用金紫銅、元明皆以胡銅為之、今亦同又有鐵製、附耳者、其形大小雖詳於居家必備、倣二人任之所用、
本國有水瓶、其形各異、間有銅鐵、或花紋禽獸鑄之、又有真鍮白銅者、肖南蠻之製、胡銅者其次也、
本邦用陶器出於伊賀信樂備前唐津且京師東乾山亦造之、然經緯剛柔之理不能得其趣又曰有染付之製、摸朝鮮白銅又其次也、
村之製、草木山澤花鳥雲堂之屬、間亦加金銀、以鉛鑞之溪土器亦然、其尨膚青白者皆雪脚不浮也、

器用部十　溪浴具一

五六九

Sample page of Koji ruien

Naomi Fukuda's *Bibliography of Reference Works for Japanese Studies*, or ask the Japanese librarian of your East Asian collection.

Since compiling an encyclopedia is an expensive endeavor, they are revised less frequently than dictionaries. To supplement encyclopedias, many publishers produce yearbooks, usually called *hyakka nenkan*, to keep the information up-to-date. For more current information, check newspapers, weekly and monthly magazines, government publications such as *hakusho* 白書 (annual summaries of various governmental agencies and other government institutions), *kanpō* 官報, and reduced versions of newspapers. Yearbooks such as *Asahi nenkan* 朝日年鑑 or *Mainichi nenkan* 毎日年鑑, published by various newspaper publishers, are also useful. For statistics, *Nihon tōkei nenkan* 日本統計年鑑 is particularly useful.

Often more than one dictionary or encyclopedia can be used to solve the problems and quizzes listed in this section. Try to use as many dictionaries, general encyclopedias, and subject encyclopedias as possible in order to become acquainted with them.

Quiz VII-2. I want to find an explanation of *ema* 絵馬 and *omamori* お守り, and their origins.

Quiz VII-3. What, other than *matsukaze* 松風, are the six sounds of boiling tea kettles?

Quiz VII-4. What is *tsukesage* 付けさげ, and what is *rinzu* りんず? I think that both are terms for clothing.

IMPORTANT DICTIONARIES AND ENCYCLOPEDIAS
DISCUSSED IN THIS CHAPTER

VII-1. Morohashi Tetsuji. *Dai Kan-Wa jiten*. Shūteiban. Tokyo: Taishūkan Shoten, 1986. 13v.

VII-2. Tōyō Gakujutsu Kenkyūjo. *Dai Kan-Wa jiten. Goi sakuin*. Tokyo: Taishūkan Shoten, 1990. 8, 56, 1,248p.

VII-3. Morohashi Tetsuji, Kamada Tadashi, and Yoneyama Toratarō. *Kō Kan-Wa jiten*. Tokyo: Taishūkan Shoten, 1981–82. 4v.

VII-4. Kamada Tadashi and Yoneyama Toratarō. *Dai Kangorin*. Tokyo: Taishūkan Shoten, 1992. 94, 1,805p.

VII-5. *Dai Kangorin goi sōran*. Tokyo: Taishūkan Shoten, 1992. 390p.

VII-6. Ueda Kazutoshi, ed. *Daijiten*, 7th ed. Tokyo: Kōdansha, 1963. 2,821p.

VII-7. Ueda Kazutoshi et al., eds. *Shin Daijiten*. Tokyo: Kōdansha, 1993. 174, 2,776, 94p.

VII-8. Nakayama Yasumasa. *Nankun jiten*. Tokyo: Tōkyōdō Shuppan, 1956. 579p.

VII-9. Spahn, Mark, Wolfgang Hadamitzky, and Kimiko Fujie-Winter. *Kan-Ei jukugo ribaasu jiten*. Tokyo: Nichigai Asoshieitsu, 1989. xviii, 1,669p.

VII-10. *Nihongo daijiten*. Tokyo: Kōdansha, 1989. 2,302p.

VII-11. *Nihon kokugo daijiten*. Tokyo: Shōgakkan, 1972–76. 20v.

VII-12. Nakamura Yukihiko, Okami Masao, and Sakakura Atsuyoshi. *Kadokawa kogo daijiten*. Tokyo: Kadokawa Shoten, 1982–.

VII-13. Ōno Susumu, Sataka Akihiro, and Maeda Kingorō. *Iwanami kogo jiten*. Tokyo: Iwanami Shoten, 1975. 1,506p.

VII-14. Maeda Isamu. *Edogo daijiten*. Tokyo: Kōdansha, 1974. 1,078p.

VII-15. *Gendai yōgo no kiso chishiki*. Tokyo: Jiyū Kokuminsha, 1948–. Annual.

VII-16. *Jōhō chishiki imidas*. Tokyo: Shūeisha, 1987–. Annual.

VII-17. *Asahi Shinbun gendai yōgo Chiezō*. Tokyo: Asahi Shinbunsha, 1990–. Annual.

VII-18. Arakawa Sōbei. *Kadokawa gairaigo jiten*, 2d ed. Tokyo: Kadokawa Shoten, 1977. 1,643p.

VII-19. *Nihon hōgen daijiten.* Tokyo: Shōgakkan, 1989. 3v.

VII-20. Nippon Hōsō Kyōkai. *Nihongo hatsuon akusento jiten,* rev. ed. Tokyo: Nippon Hōsō Shuppan Kyōkai, 1985. 990, 204p.

VII-21. Umegaki Minoru. *Ingo jiten.* Tokyo: Tōkyōdō, 1956. 16, 600p.

VII-22. Ōno Susumu and Hamanishi Masando. *Kadokawa ruigo shinjiten.* Tokyo: Kadokawa Shoten, 1981. 932p.

VII-23. Shiraishi Daiji. *Giseigo gitaigo kan'yōku jiten.* Tokyo: Tōkyōdō Shuppan, 1982. 668p.

VII-24. Muraishi Toshio. *Nihongo gogen jiten.* Tokyo: Nihon Bungeisha, 1981. 444p.

VII-25. Shōgaku Tosho, ed. *Koji zokushin kotowaza daijiten.* Tokyo: Shōgakkan, 1982. 13, 1,998p.

VII-26. *Seigorin: Koji kotowaza kan'yōku.* Tokyo: Obunsha, 1992. 1v. with supplement.

VII-27. *Sekai daihyakka jiten.* Tokyo: Heibonsha, 1988. 35v.

VII-28. Jingū Shichō. *Koji ruien.* Tokyo: Yoshikawa Kōbunkan, 1967-72. 51v.

VII-29. *Kodansha Encyclopedia of Japan.* Tokyo and New York: Kodansha International, 1983. 9v. plus supplement.

Chapter Eight
Gazetteers and Historical Atlases

Geographical names are at least as difficult to handle as people's names. They are often irregular in reading, and even innocent-looking names written in plain Chinese characters turn out to be tricky and have to be read in almost unimaginable ways such as 及位 "Nozoki" and 間人 "Taiza." Additionally, there is the problem of multiple readings such as "Hinata," "Hiyomo," "Hyūga," "Himuki," "Himukai," "Hinada," "Nikkō," and more for the Chinese characters 日向. Even if you know how the Chinese characters can be read, you still have to pinpoint the correct reading for that particular place-name. There are also a number of place-names that use characters with many strokes. They are so difficult to decipher that even the government tried to change them by law in 1962 to simpler characters. Using a map to locate a place-name is often not enough, particularly when the name happens to be historical or is not in use any longer. Gazetteers are used in these cases because they tend to include more names with detailed information about the place and to list historical changes. For information beyond Papinot's *Historical and Geographical Dictionary of Japan,* which is a helpful, basic resource, you need to search farther afield for Japanese-language gazetteers.

Gendai Nihon chimei yomikata daijiten 現代日本地名よみかた大辞典 (VIII-1) in seven volumes includes 310,000 names selected out of 420,000 from the largest to the smallest geographical unit. It is arranged by the stroke count of the first character of the name and shows the readings and the location of each name. Each entry is numbered. The index volume is arranged by the common *on* reading and leads one to the correct entry. This completely new type of reference book has almost entirely solved the difficult problems we have had to face when dealing with geographical names. It can be used to read practically every name, to learn the different possible readings for a combination of Chinese characters, to find the location of a particular name, and to find the locations of geographical names written with the same Chinese characters. All the inconveniences and guesswork related to geographical names have disappeared thanks to this phenomenal work.

Chimei yomikata jiten 地名よみかた辞典 (VIII-2), an affordable one-volume dictionary of geographical names, was prepared from *Gendai Nihon chimei yomikata daijiten* by selecting 50,000 hard-to-read place-names, mostly heavily populated cities and suburbs, and then adding 6,000 commonly seen names of mountains, rivers, lakes, coastlines, islands, railroads, and roads, as well as historical place-names. The arrangement of the entries and the index is the same as the arrangement in *Gendai Nihon chimei yomikata daijiten*. For place-names outside Japan and written in Chinese characters, see *Chū-Nichi-Ō taishō sekai chimei jinmei jiten* (VI-6).

Nihon chimei sakuin 日本地名索引 (VIII-3) can be used in a similar fashion as *Gendai Nihon chimei yomikata daijiten*, but it was actually intended to improve the user's ability to find the exact location of a geographical name on a map. Indexes to geographical names include a historical place-name index and an index to specific locations on standardized maps.

Use geographical dictionaries to find more detailed information, such as change of name, change of administrative division, and more. *Nihon rekishi chimei taikei* 日本歴史地名大系 (VIII-4) is an encyclopedic collection of Japanese geographical names from the beginning of the country. Entries include archaeological sites, ruins of castles, temples, bridges, and names no longer in existence. Names from basic source materials, local documents, and legends also appear. In general, each volume is assigned to a prefecture. Kyoto City (municipality) has an independent volume. This work is meant to replace Yoshida's *Dai Nihon chimei jisho*, which is over eighty years old, by including the latest findings of interdisciplinary scholarship, local historians, and archaeological excavations. Approximately 200,000 entries are included. One of the unique characteristics of this work is that for every prefecture an editorial committee was formed mainly by local historians and specialists. Each volume includes an introduction, place-name section, bibliographic references, lists of annotations for important sources for the study of local history,

かでん	下田	〔1435〕	がと	芽登	〔27949〕
	下佃	〔1510〕	がど	瓦土	〔14004〕
	下殿	〔1982〕	かとう	下冬	〔1399〕
	下鮎	〔2113〕		下当	〔1488〕
	戈田	〔9085〕		下豆	〔1562〕
	加田	〔10901〕		下沓	〔1618〕
	加殿	〔10973〕		下東	〔1621〕
	瓜田	〔18448〕		下到	〔1645〕
	花田	〔22406〕		下唐	〔1738〕
	花殿	〔22502〕		下島	〔1743〕
	河田	〔26977〕		下桐	〔1756〕
	夏田	〔34448〕		下桃	〔1762〕
	家田	〔34545〕		下桶	〔1837〕
	荷田	〔36981〕		下塔	〔1895〕

1743 下島：くだりしま（愛知県蒲郡市水竹町下島：ガマゴオリシ　ミズタケチョウ）
　　下島：げしま（愛知県丹羽郡大口町大字小口字下島：ニワグン　オオグチチョウチ）
　　下島：したじま（富山県東礪波郡上平村下島：ヒガシトナミグン　カミタイラムラ）
　　下島：したじま（長野県木曽郡日義村下島：キソグン　ヒヨシムラ）
　　下島：しもじま（福島県伊達郡梁川町大字二野袋字下島：ダテグン　ヤナガワマチノフクロ）
　　下島：しもじま（茨城県筑波郡伊奈村大字下島：ツクバグン　イナムラ）
　　下島：しもじま（神奈川県平塚市下島：ヒラツカシ）
　　下島：しもじま（新潟県北魚沼郡堀之内町大字下島：キタウオヌマグン　ホリノウ）
　　下島：しもじま（富山県滑川市下島：ナメリカワシ）

Sample page of Gendai Nihon chimei yomikata daijiten

gazetteers and maps, changes of administrative boundaries, and an index arranged in Japanese syllabary order.

Kadokawa Nihon chimei daijiten 角川日本地名大辞典 (VIII-5), a similar publication to *Nihon rekishi chimei taikei*, also assigns a volume to each prefecture. Volumes consist of four parts: general, geographical names, gazetteers, and sources. In *Chimei hen*, both administrative place-names arranged according to historical order and other names are included as entry words. Because of its specific focus on ancient, medieval, and premodern names, this encyclopedic gazetteer is particularly useful for Japanese studies. It not only supplements the uneven coverage of Yoshida's *Dai Nihon chimei jisho* but also contains far more entries (40,000 versus 500,000). Sources are included.

Dai Nihon chimei jisho 大日本地名辞書 (VIII-6) in eight volumes has been a monumental Japanese geographical dictionary based on historical principles since its first publication in 1911–13. A revised edition was published during 1969–71. Besides place-names, it also includes the names of famous temples, rivers, mountains, and landmarks. A detailed explanation is included under each entry. There are some limitations for the choice of entry words because it was based mostly on *Wamyō ruijushō* 和名類聚抄 and because of its age; still, it is a must because of its coverage of territory beyond present Japan, including information on Sakhalin and Taiwan. It contains information from sources such as *Azuma kagami* 東鑑, *Kojiki* 古事記, and other older historical sources including numerous books on local history. It contains a good general introduction to the whole subject of Japanese geography and also detailed indexes arranged both in Japanese syllabary order and by the stroke count of the first Chinese character of the entry word.

There are various kinds of thematic maps and atlases available. *Nihon rekishi chizu* 日本歴史地図 (VIII-7) is an enlarged, revised edition of a historical atlas with the same title that was compiled and published in one volume in 1956. The original has been a standard historical atlas for many years. This new, enlarged edition is much more detailed, however, incorporating recent achievements of scholarship in this subject area. It includes many introductory essays for each section along with, of course, numerous maps and photographic illustrations, all in color. This is a good marriage of the characteristics of Yoshida's *Dai Nihon dokushi chizu* and the 1956 edition of *Nihon rekishi chizu*. It is divided into *Genshi kodai hen* 原始古代編, *Chūsei hen* 中世編, and *Kinsei hen* 近世編. Each volume has indexes arranged by stroke count and in Japanese syllabary order. The 1956 edition and *Nihon rekishi chizu,* a supplement volume of *Nihon rekishi daijiten,* should be used until this extensive revision is completed.

Shin Nihon bunken chizu 新日本分県地図 (VIII-8), the successor to *Dai Nihon bunken chizu*, contains for each prefecture a detailed map, a list of administrative subdivisions and geographical names, and a list of public offices and service agencies. Supplements, such as railroad maps and distance tables for automobiles, are included. The strong point of this work is that it has various indexes for geographical names, including rivers, islands, lakes, and mountains, in addition to regular place-names. *Nihon bunken chizu chimei sōran* 日本分県地図地名総覧 is very similar, and both are revised and published annually.

When you are looking for a specific map that cannot be found in either one of the works mentioned above, bibliographies of maps, such as *Kokuritsu Kokkai Toshokan shozō chizu mokuroku* 国立国会図書館所蔵地図目録 (VIII-9), are available. If you need sources on a specific local area, *Chihōshi bunken sōgō mokuroku* 地方史文献総合目録 (VIII-10) compiled by Atsusaka Rintarō should be consulted.

Quiz VIII-1. I want to find the geographical and cultural background of Senju 千住 during the Edo period. Senju is mentioned in *Oku no hosomichi* by Matsuo Bashō.

Quiz VIII-2. I am going to Nirayama 韮山 in Shizuoka Prefecture. Where can I find information about that town? Is there a train station near by?

Quiz VIII-3. During the Meiji era there were several publishers in Ushigome-ku, Tōkyō-fu 東京府牛込区. Where was it and what is the place called now?

Quiz VIII-4. Can you find any city plans of Heijōkyō 平城京 or Fujiwarakyō 藤原京?

IMPORTANT GAZETTEERS AND ATLASES DISCUSSED IN THIS CHAPTER

VIII-1. *Gendai Nihon chimei yomikata daijiten*. Tokyo: Nichigai Asoshieitsu, 1985. 6v. and index.

VIII-2. *Chimei yomikata jiten*. Tokyo: Nichigai Asoshieitsu, 1989. xvi, 855, 132p.

VIII-3. Kanai Hiroo. *Nihon chimei sakuin*. Kamakura: Abokkusha, 1981. 2v.

VIII-4. *Nihon rekishi chimei taikei*. Tokyo: Heibonsha, 1979–. 49v. and index.

VIII-5. *Kadokawa Nihon chimei daijiten*. Tokyo: Kadokawa Shoten, 1978–. 47v. and index.

VIII-6. Yoshida Tōgo. *Dai Nihon chimei jisho*, rev. and enl. ed. Tokyo: Fuzanbō, 1969–71. 8v.

VIII-7. *Nihon rekishi chizu* (The historical atlas of Japan). Tokyo: Kashiwa Shobō, 1982–. 2v. and continuing.

VIII-8. *Shin Nihon bunken chizu*. Tokyo: Kokusai Chigaku Kyōkai, 1969–. Annual.

VIII-9. *Kokuritsu Kokkai Toshokan shozō chizu mokuroku*. Tokyo: Kokuritsu Kokkai Toshokan, 1966–.

VIII-10. Atsusaka Rintarō, comp. *Chihōshi bunken sōgō mokuroku*. Tokyo: Gannandō Shoten, 1970–75. 3v.

Chapter Nine
Calendars and Chronologies

1. CALENDARS

Japan used a lunar calendar until the Meiji government adopted the Gregorian calendar on January 1, 1873. As their normal method for identifying dates, Japanese now use either the Western calendar or the month and day of the Western calendar combined with a calendrical era known as a *nengō* 年号. *Heisei 3-nen 1-gatsu tsuitachi* means New Year's Day of the third year of Heisei, that is, January 1, 1991. *Nengō*, the era name, originated in China in 140 B.C., and Japan and Korea adopted it from China (using names based on either good omens or the Chinese classics). Era names were decided on by officials and were often changed, even during a single emperor's reign, because of good or ill luck. The earliest official use of *nengō* in Japan was A.D. 645 during the reign of Empress Kōtoku as Taika. Before the Meiji period, the *nengō* was often changed when a new emperor's reign began or in certain years in the sexagenary cycle, based on ancient Chinese astrological principles. During the time of the Southern and Northern courts, both courts used different *nengō*. Among the common people, private *nengō* (*shinengō* 私年号 or *ginengō* 偽年号), which were created in the medieval period, were used along with or parallel to the official *nengō*. Chinese characters meaning good luck were chosen for this. Sometimes the news of a change in the name of the era did not spread fast enough, and occasionally local governments in particular continued to use *nengō* no longer in official use. Be cautious, particularly when the change in era name came toward the end of the year, such as Tenpō 天保. The thirteenth year of Bunsei 文政 was changed to the first year of Tenpō on the tenth day of twelfth month (equivalent to January 23, 1831 in the Gregorian calendar), and some local documents have been found with a date of the fourteenth year of Bunsei, which did not exist. Although since the

Meiji era only one *nengō* has been allowed for each emperor's reign, the fifteenth year of Taishō ended on December 25, 1926, and thus the last few days of December became first year of Shōwa. The January issue of *Nihon oyobi Nihonjin* was dated in the sixteenth year of Taishō instead of the second year of Shōwa because it had already been printed when Emperor Taishō passed away. Since the Meiji era (1868–), a *nengō* corresponds to the entire reign of an emperor, but before then, *nengō* were changed frequently for various reasons and have no significant meaning.

1868.10.23
Meiji 1   45
            1912.7.30
            Taishō 1   15
                         1926.12.25
                         Shōwa 1   64
                                     1989.1.7
                                     Heisei 1

When you deal with calendrical dates before January 1873, conversion is tricky and complex. We urge you to read chapter 2, "Problems Concerning Dates, Time, and Chronology" in Webb's book. Oriental calendars are very complex because of the use of various systems at the same time. One system is the Western solar-based system; a second is the Chinese lunar system, which uses sexagenary cycles; and a third utilizes *nengō*, Japanese era names. Yet another system of numbering years, which is no longer in use, is *kōki* 皇紀, based on the mythical origin of Japan (660 B.C. is considered to be year one). Use one of the following chronological conversion tables when the need arises.

Hōreki seireki taishōhyō 邦暦西暦対照表 (IX-1), a bilingual chronological table covering the years from A.D. 601 to 1872, compares the Western calendar with the Japanese calendar and the sexagenary cycle. It is convenient and very easy to use. For each Western calendar year, there is a table containing information on the corresponding year of the imperial reign, the year according to the *nengō* system together with the sexagenary sign of the year, and the sexagenary character of the first day of the first month according to the lunar calendar. Figures in Gothic type refer to months of thirty days; figures in Roman type refer to months of twenty-nine days. A figure in italic type means that the month is an intercalary one. An appendix has various conversion tables, including a table for computing the sexagenary signs.

Nihon in'yō rekijitsu taishōhyō 日本陰陽暦日対照表 (IX-2) is a day-to-day table converting the lunar calendar to the Western calendar from A.D. 445 to 1872. The work of Kakara Kōzaburō took fifteen years to produce. Tsuchihashi's *Hōreki seireki taishōhyō* covers a much shorter period but is bilingual and therefore convenient for English-language speakers.

Nihon rekijitsu genten 日本暦日原典 (IX-3) is designed to correct the mistakes in *Sansei sōran* 三正綜覧 (IX-4), the most widely used table for finding calendar days, which is based on an inaccurate work, *Kōwa tsūreki* 皇和通暦 by Nakane Genkei. It is divided into two parts: *rekijitsu hen*, a table of the lunar calendar and the Western calendar, and *rekihō hen*, which is the explanation of how the table works. In *rekijitsu hen*, all the days and years from A.D. 445 to 1872, when Japan switched to using the Western calendar, are determined and shown in both Japanese and the Western calendars using calculations based on the rules of a lunar calendar. Information included for each year is the *nengō*, the sexagenary date, and the number of days in that lunar year. Information included for each month is the number of days, the sexagenary sign of the first day of the lunar month, the Western date, and so on.

Chronological conversion tables, which cover shorter periods of time, can be found for various historical periods or subject areas. One good example of such a work is *Nihonreki seireki gappi taishōhyō* 日本暦西暦月日対照表 (IX-5), which covers the years from 1582 to 1872, including the whole Edo period. Each page represents a whole year, and in one look at the table the user can tell the date, either from lunar to Western calendar or vice versa, and the day of the month.

Jikkan 十干 (which are the ten calendar signs such as 甲 [*kō* = *kinoe*], 乙 [*otsu* = *kinoto*], and 丙 [*hei* = *hinoe*]) and *jūnishi* 十二支 (which are the twelve signs such as 子 [*shi* = *ne*], 丑 [*chū* = *ushi*], and 寅 [*in* = *tora*]) are combined to create the sexagenary cycle or zodiac signs, a sixty-year cycle starting with *kinoene*. You can find which year corresponds to which zodiac sign in any chronological table. Some combinations of *eto* 干支, which is a combination of *jikkan* and *jūnishi*, are associated with certain personality character-

慶長6年（辛丑） ↓ 1601年

⑪月	旧	1 2 3 4 5 6 7	一六〇二年	8 9 10 11	27 28 29
	新	12		1	
		25 26 27 28 29 30 31		1 2 3 4	20 21 22
	曜	火 水 木 金 土 日 月		火 水 木 金	日 月 火

→表より、慶長6年（辛丑）閏11月8日は西暦1602年1月1日㈫である。

III. 対照上の注意点

1. 日本暦は1ヵ月30日迄の月を〈大の月〉と称し、29日迄の月を〈小の月〉という。
2. 日本暦の閏月は、日本暦を調整するため、32～35ヵ月ごとに、1ヵ月（大の月の30日、または小の月の29日）を1年に加え、1年を13ヵ月としている。
3. 西洋暦（グレゴリオ暦）は、1582年10月15日に実施されたが、これはその年の10月4日の翌日を15日としたもので、5～14日の日付がない。
4. 西洋暦においては、1年を$365\frac{2425}{}$日とするため、4年に1度の閏年を設け、2月29日を閏日としているが、400年に3回（1700、1800、1900年の各年にあたる）省略することにし、400年で割れる年（1600、2000年）は省略しないこととしている。
5. 日本は1873年(明治6年)1月1日から西洋暦を採用したが、明治5年12月4日から30日までの旧暦日はない。

1860年 閏年　　　安政7・万延元年（庚申）

1月	旧	1	2	3	4	5	6	7	8	9	10	11	12	13	14	15	16	17	18	19	20	21	22	23	24	25	26	27	28	29	30
	新	1											2																			
		23	24	25	26	27	28	29	30	31	1	2	3	4	5	6	7	8	9	10	11	12	13	14	15	16	17	18	19	20	21
	曜	月	火	水	木	金	土	日	月	火	水	木	金	土	日	月	火	水	木	金	土	日	月	火	水	木	金	土	日	月	火

（以下同様の表が2月、3月、閏3月、4月と続く）

Sample page of Nihonreki seireki gappi taishōhyō

istics of the people who are born in that particular year. For example, 1846, 1906, and 1966, the year of *hinoeuma* 丙午, recorded a smaller population increase than other years, particularly in the numbers of reported births of baby girls. The reason for this is that there is a superstition that women born in the year of *hinoeuma* are headstrong and eat up their husbands. Amazingly, this superstition was still believed by many, so that it affected the birthrate of 1966.

This same *jūnishi* system is also used to tell the time of the day, *ne* being 12:00 midnight, as well as to indicate directions (see the illustration below). Read chapter 2 of Webb's book for a detailed explanation.

Quiz IX-1. What was the date, in the Western calendar, of the start of the Boshin War 戊辰戦争?

Quiz IX-2. How old are the people who were born in the most recent year of *kinoesaru* 甲申? When would they celebrate their *kanreki* 還暦 (the sixtieth anniversary of their birth)?

Quiz IX-3. What direction is *tatsumi no kata* 巽の方?

Quiz IX-4. What time is *ushimitsudoki* 丑満刻 or 丑三つ時?

2. CHRONOLOGIES

Nenpyō Nihon rekishi 年表日本歴史 (IX-6) will be the most extensive chronological table when completed. Each volume has a discussion of the period followed by chronological tables, various lists, and an extensive index arranged in Japanese syllabary order. Entries are divided into three regions, with detailed footnotes. Volume 1 covers the period up to A.D. 783 (Genshi or prehistoric, Asuka, and Nara 原始 飛鳥 奈良); volume 2 covers the years A.D. 784 to 1184 (Heian 平安); volume 3 covers 1185 to 1567 (Kamakura and Muromachi 鎌倉 室町); and volume 4 covers 1568 to 1715 (Azuchi Momoyama and the first half of the Edo period 安土 桃山 江戸前期). Volumes 5 and 6 are projected to cover the later Edo period 江戸後期 to the Shōwa era 昭和.

Nihon rekishi nenpyō 日本歴史年表 (IX-7) is a supplementary volume of *Nihon rekishi daijiten* 日本歴史大辞典. It covers the

CALENDARS AND CHRONOLOGIES

干支順位表/方位・時刻表 —1124—

干支順位表

甲子 きのえね カッシ	乙丑 きのとうし イッチュウ	丙寅 ひのえとら ヘイイン	丁卯 ひのとう テイボウ	戊辰 つちのえたつ ボシン	己巳 つちのとみ キシ	庚午 かのえうま コウゴ	辛未 かのとひつじ シンビ	壬申 みずのえさる ジンシン	癸酉 みずのととり キユウ
甲戌 きのえいぬ コウジュツ	乙亥 きのとい イツガイ	丙子 ひのえね ヘイシ	丁丑 ひのとうし テイチュウ	戊寅 つちのえとら ボイン	己卯 つちのとう キボウ	庚辰 かのえたつ コウシン	辛巳 かのとみ シンシ	壬午 みずのえうま ジンゴ	癸未 みずのとひつじ キビ
甲申 きのえさる コウシン	乙酉 きのととり イツユウ	丙戌 ひのえいぬ ヘイジュツ	丁亥 ひのとい テイガイ	戊子 つちのえね ボシ	己丑 つちのとうし キチュウ	庚寅 かのえとら コウイン	辛卯 かのとう シンボウ	壬辰 みずのえたつ ジンシン	癸巳 みずのとみ キシ
甲午 きのえうま コウゴ	乙未 きのとひつじ イツビ	丙申 ひのえさる ヘイシン	丁酉 ひのととり テイユウ	戊戌 つちのえいぬ ボジュツ	己亥 つちのとい キガイ	庚子 かのえね コウシ	辛丑 かのとうし シンチュウ	壬寅 みずのえとら ジンイン	癸卯 みずのとう キボウ
甲辰 きのえたつ コウシン	乙巳 きのとみ イッシ	丙午 ひのえうま ヘイゴ	丁未 ひのとひつじ テイビ	戊申 つちのえさる ボシン	己酉 つちのととり キユウ	庚戌 かのえいぬ コウジュツ	辛亥 かのとい シンガイ	壬子 みずのえね ジンシ	癸丑 みずのとうし キチュウ
甲寅 きのえとら コウイン	乙卯 きのとう イツボウ	丙辰 ひのえたつ ヘイシン	丁巳 ひのとみ テイシ	戊午 つちのえうま ボゴ	己未 つちのとひつじ キビ	庚申 かのえさる コウシン	辛酉 かのととり シンユウ	壬戌 みずのえいぬ ジンジュツ	癸亥 みずのとい キガイ

方位・時刻表

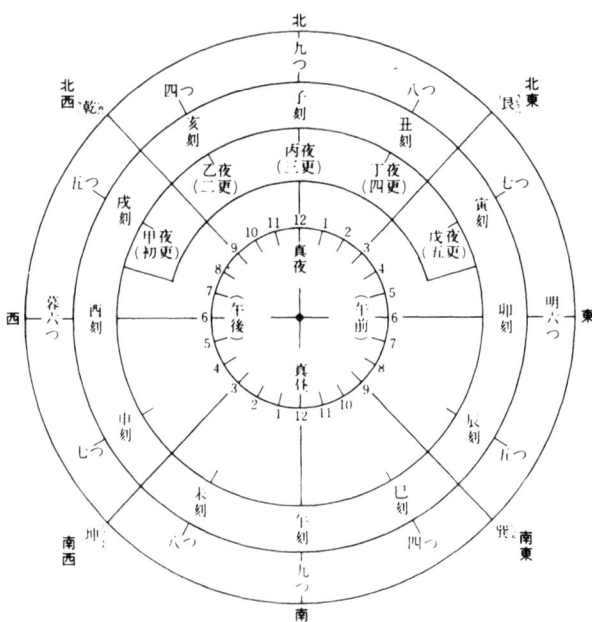

Eto, Time and Directions

time from A.D. 1 to 1959. A chronology section for each year includes the Western calendar year, name of the sexagenary cyclic sign, era name, emperor, and chief adviser to the emperor. Later, names of shogun and main information columns are divided into politics, economics, and society and culture, with their dates (according to the lunar calendar to 1872). It lacks an index. This book is updated by the same group that produced *Nihon shi nenpyō* 新版日本史年表 (IX-8). Another *Nihon shi nenpyō* 新版日本史年表 (IX-9), which received a complete revision from its earlier edition in 1966, became even more convenient and useful with the addition of a general index for 4,000 important words. The index solved the problems and frustrations of flipping through many pages, and it is a tremendous timesaver. Any frequent user of chronological tables knows how convenient this is. This edition also includes various useful appendixes, and a *nengō* index is printed on the endpapers of the book. The main text is divided into three sections: politics and economics, society and culture, and the world. Another small but good new work is *Nihon shi nenpyō* 日本史年表 (IX-10), which gives sources of information for entries before the Edo period. Important entries are in Gothic type, and the division of topics changes with the needs of each period. It has various tables appended but has no index except one for *nengō*.

Kindai Nihon sōgō nenpyō 近代日本総合年表 (IX-11) covers the period from 1853, the year when Perry's "Black ships" came to Japan, through 1989. It is divided into six sections: politics; economics; industries and technology; society; academics, education and thought; and foreign countries. Sometimes the same topics are divided among these sections, so the user should be cautious. For example, Shinto and Buddhism are treated in both the society and academic columns; new religions are treated in the society column; and Christianity is treated in the academic column. Important events are printed in bold type. For each column, important events, trends, and other information are listed under *kono toshi*, "this year." Many entries list sources in numerical order at the end, and all sources are numerically listed at the end of the volume before the general index, which is arranged in Japanese syllabary order.

Nihon bunka sōgō nenpyō 日本文化総合年表 (IX-12) focuses on cultural aspects of Japanese history, from ancient times to 1988. Here "culture" is used in its broadest sense and includes politics, society, academics, religion, arts, and literature. There are 30,000 entry words, many of them unique in this chronology, which uses authoritative sources. Each entry includes sources up to the medieval period. Equipped with a detailed general index, it is an extremely important and handy reference, particularly for users in the humanities. There are many smaller general chronological tables, but few deserve special mention here.

There are also numerous subject chronologies available. We will discuss only a few of the examples. *Nihon bungaku dainenpyō* 日本文学大年表 (IX-13) is a chronology of literary works and people, including translations, foreign literature, art and literary criticism, dramas, and journals. Events of a general nature are also included. For each year in the Western calendar, the name of the emperor, shogun, or others who held administrative positions and the *nengō* are given. Each section changes from period to period to reflect the emphasis of the literary world of the time. For example, entries of subjects before the Edo period are divided into four sections: literature, others, people, and events of a general nature. Entries of subjects during the Edo period are divided into six sections: *waka* and *haikai*, novels and plays, Chinese-style poetry and others, people, foreign literature, and general. Entries for the Meiji era are also divided into six sections, but a little differently: poetry, novels and plays, criticism, people and events, foreign literature, and events of a general nature. Extensive indexes for people and titles of works and journals are the strength of this chronology. As the title indicates, *Gendai Nihon bungaku nenpyō* 現代日本文学年表 is another literary chronology for a specific period. *Genshoku zuten Nihon bijutsushi nenpyō* 原色図典日本美術史年表 (IX-14) has many illustrations in color, and this visual approach is very helpful for understanding Japanese art history. It selects important information for architecture, sculpture, paintings, fine arts, and calligraphy. It includes the sources of information and a general index.

Quiz IX-5. When the first governmental mission to Europe (第一回 遣欧使節 , one of the members was Fukuzawa Yukichi) came back, what kind of political and social incidents had happened and were about to happen in and around Edo?

CHAPTER NINE

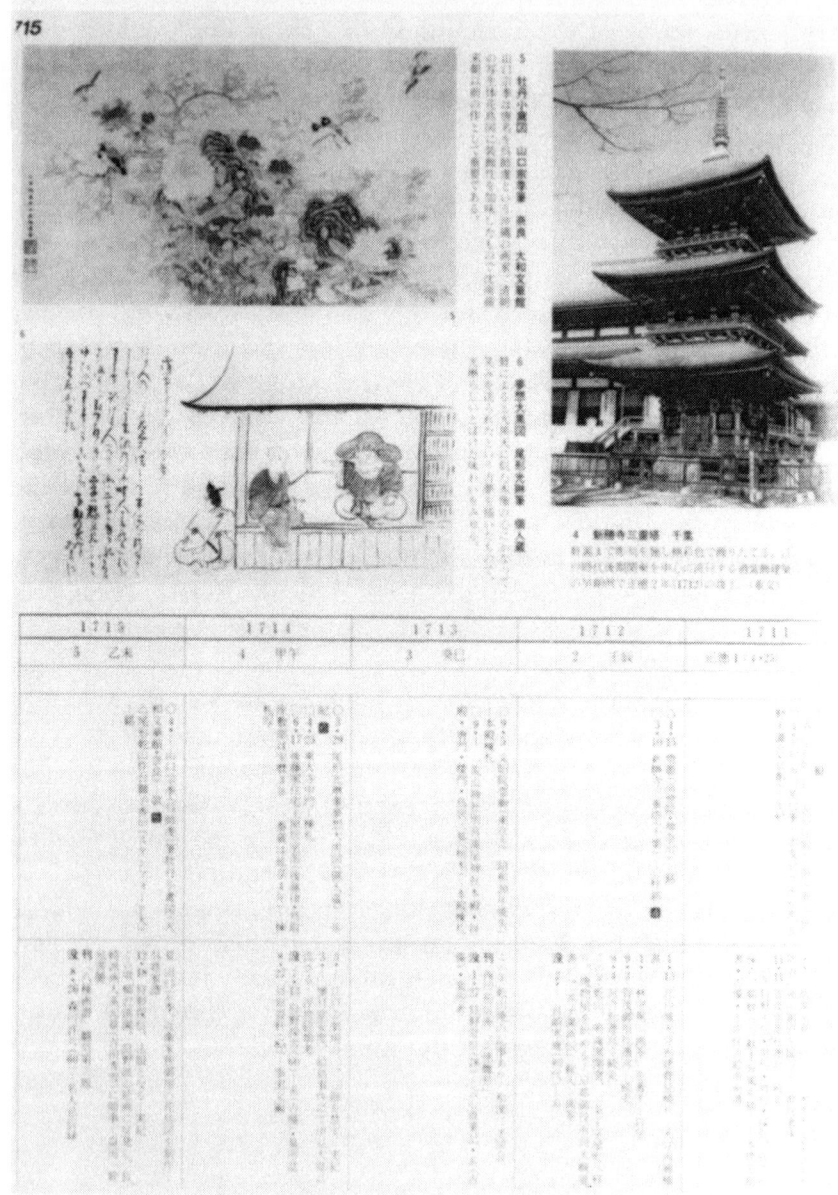

Sample page of Genshoku zuten Nihon bijutsushi nenpyō

CALENDARS AND CHRONOLOGIES 113

IMPORTANT CALENDARS AND CHRONOLOGICAL
TABLES DISCUSSED IN THIS CHAPTER

IX-1. Tsuchihashi Yachita. *Hōreki seireki taishōhyō* (Japanese chronological tables from A.D. 601 to 1872). Monumenta Nipponica Monographs, no.11. Tokyo: Sophia University Press, 1952. 128p.

IX-2. Kakara Kōzaburō. *Nihon in'yō rekijitsu taishōhyō*. Tokyo: Nittō, 1991–93. 2v.

IX-3. Uchida Masao. *Nihon rekijitsu genten*, 4th ed. Tokyo: Yūzankaku Shuppan, 1992. xi, 560p.

IX-4. Naimushō Chirikyoku. *Sansei sōran*, rev. and corrected ed. Kamakura: Geirinsha, 1973. 428, 101p.

IX-5. Nojima Jusaburō. *Nihonreki seireki gappi taishōhyō 1582–1872*. Tokyo: Nichigai Asoshieitsu, 1987. 291, 12p.

IX-6. Inoue Mitsusada, Kodama Kōta, and Hayashiya Tatsusaburō. *Nenpyō Nihon rekishi*. Tokyo: Chikuma Shobō, 1980–.

IX-7. Naramoto Tatsuya et al. *Nihon rekishi nenpyō*. Supplement to *Nihon rekishi daijiten*. Tokyo: Kawade Shobō Shinsha, 1960. 374, 59p.

IX-8. Nihon Rekishi Daijiten Henshū Iinkai. *Nihon shi nenpyō*, rev. ed. Tokyo: Kawade Shobō Shinsha, 1986. 388, 109p.

IX-9. Rekishigaku Kenkyūkai. *Nihon shi nenpyō*, rev. ed. Tokyo: Iwanami Shoten, 1984. vi, 389p.

IX-10. Tōkyō Gakugei Daigaku Nihonshi Kenkyūshitsu. *Nihon shi nenpyō*. Tokyo: Tōkyōdō Shuppan, 1990. 4, 536p.

IX-11. Iwanami Shoten Henshūbu. *Kindai Nihon sōgō nenpyō*, 3d ed. Tokyo: Iwanami Shoten, 1991. x, 736p.

IX-12. Ichiko Teiji et al. *Nihon bunka sōgō nenpyō*. Tokyo: Iwanami Shoten, 1990. v, 596p.

IX-13. Ichiko Teiji. *Nihon bungaku dainenpyō*. Tokyo: Ōfūsha, 1986. 515p.

IX-14. Ōta Hirotarō et al. *Genshoku zuten Nihon bijutsushi nenpyō*. Tokyo: Shūeisha, 1986. xi, 563p.

Chapter Ten
Japanese Literature

It is beyond the scope of this small guide to cover the thousands of reference works and bibliographies for all fields of Japanese studies, and thus we have selected the subject area of "literature" to treat in a fairly detailed manner. We urge you to carry out a similar bibliographic search as the one here using the guides to reference works that we discussed in chapter five.

Until now we have studied representative general bibliographies and other reference works. If you had already decided on your topic and used some of those bibliographies and indexes, you probably found enough materials. Why bother to repeat the process here? Why do people take the trouble to compile subject bibliographies? Because subject bibliographies are exclusive rather than inclusive and are much more detailed than general bibliographies and reference works. Subject bibliographies can also include materials that could be easily missed by general bibliographies. They can be comprehensive or selective, critical and evaluative, and informative on more obscure materials such as parts of books, periodical articles, pamphlets, and papers presented at conferences. They are much more convenient for specialists and students in the field to use and are often arranged by narrower divisions in the subject area. Once you learn to use subject bibliographies in your field, the normal procedure is to start your search using them rather than the general bibliographies. This does not in any way belittle the importance of general bibliographies. They are very useful for bibliographic searches when no subject bibliography is available, for supplementing the outdated subject bibliographies, or for searching interdisciplinary topics.

1. LOCATING INDIVIDUAL WORKS

The general bibliographies in chapter one from *Kokusho sōmokuroku* (I-16) to *Nihon zenkoku shoshi shūkanban* (I-24) should be used for finding works in independent book form. For works that were included in literary collections or monographic series, use *Zenshū sōsho saimoku sōran: Koten hen* 全集叢書細目総覧：古典編 (X-1). *Koten hen* includes individual titles of Japanese classics from 1868 to 1985 that appear in collected works, monographic series published in regular book format and mimeograph format, and reprints and that are owned mostly by the National Diet Library. Large collections published in microform are also included. It is particularly useful for discovering minor works not found elsewhere, although it excludes manuscripts, Festschrifts, *bunkobon* 文庫本, *kōza* 講座, collections of private documents, and documents and source materials of minor temples and shrines. Excluded also are collections of Buddhist sutras, paintings, maps, and music scores. It contains printed materials, including mimeographed copies or reprints. Read the *hanrei*, "explanatory notes," to find out whether *Koten hen* includes works in your area because the criteria for inclusion or exclusion are fairly complicated. The index volume includes a hard-to-read title index arranged by stroke count. *Nihon sōsho sakuin* 日本叢書索引 (X-2) is a similar work, smaller in scale.

Pre-Meiji materials that are not included in *Kokusho sōmokuroku* can probably be found in *Gunsho ruijū* 群書類従 (*sei, zoku,* and *zoku zoku*) (X-3), *Nihon zuihitsu taisei* 日本随筆大成 (X-4), and *Nihon zuihitsu sakuin* 日本随筆索引 (X-5). The last one is essentially a subject index (in *kana* syllabary order) to roughly five hundred books of essays written during the Edo period. Some typographical errors are found here and there.

Until recently, it has been a difficult and time-consuming undertaking to find individual works of modern literature that have not been published under their own titles, in part because many meticulously prepared *zenshū* ("complete works" of an author) do not have an index. You thus had to check the table of contents of each volume individually. With the publication of *Gendai Nihon bungaku sōran shiriizu* 現代日本文学綜覧シリーズ (X-6), however, the task of locating a "hidden" work has been made unbelievably easy for individual works, even poems and essays. Series 1-3 covers collected works from 1925 to 1981. Series 1, *Zenshū naiyō sōran* 全集内容綜覧, lists the table of contents of each individual volume, along with the title for each book and its date of publication. It is arranged by date of

野史台維新史料叢書 やしだいいしんしりょうそうしょ 日本史
籍協会編 昭四七―五〇 四〇冊 復製
(GB631―31)

一 公文
明治元年七月御沙汰書(東京府在勤へ) 他二三

二 論策
五編
擬対策(土屋矢之助)
土屋矢之助対策
功罪案余論(土屋矢之助)
答問十策(亀井道載)
平野次郎培覆論
真木和泉守保臣建策
極論時事封事(古賀精里)
水戸烈公戊戌封事
藤田東湖王辰封事
海防備論(藤森恭助)
神武必勝論中・下巻(平野次郎)
解腕痴言(久阪義助)
思の侭(同)
神州恢復秘策(楢崎節庵)
槊梅儲言(佐藤信淵)
薩藩功罪断案(土屋矢之助)
新政談(藤森恭助)

三 上書一
佐賀侯上書
松平主税助建白
薩州藩士申牒

松平薩摩守上書
山口薫次郎上書
松平美濃守上書
水戸烈公上九条殿下書
鷹司輔煕公上書
近衛忠煕公上書
藤田東湖封事三論
有栖川中務卿熾仁親王上書
佐久間象山上書
七卿上書
島津侯建白書
同十月十六日建白
高島喜平上書
水戸藩臣申上書
辻茂右衛門上書
吉田松陰上大原三位卿書付時勢論
池田筑後守上書
菅原薫子上書
吉田松陰将及私言
吉田松陰急務条議
近藤勇建白書
島津和泉上書
大槻磐溪上書
長州侯建白書
本田弥右衛門呈牧野備前守書
島津将監外二名上書
野城広助上沢主水正書
松平肥後守上書
浪士某等上薩州侯書
因州侯建白書
清河八郎上孝明天皇封事

四 上書二

Sample page of Zenshu sōsho saimoku sōran

CHAPTER TEN

川(岡本かの子)
　　　　　　………………新日本文学全集25(改造)昭15
　──　　……………日本短篇文学全集38(筑摩)昭43
川(新田潤)　……日本短篇文学全集44(筑摩)昭45
川(柳田国男)
　　　　　　……………現代日本文学全集12(筑摩)昭30
　──　　……………日本現代文学全集36(講談)昭43
　──　　……………現代日本文学大系20(筑摩)昭44
河(北川冬彦)
　　　　………日本プロレタリア文学大系7(三一)昭30
　──　　……………現代国民文学全集36(角川)昭33

岡本かの子全集
冬樹社
全15巻補巻1巻別巻2巻
昭和49年4月〜昭和53年3月

岡本かの子全集　1　小説　1
昭和49年9月15日

かやの生立………………………… 3
夫人と画家………………………… 22
帰去来……………………………… 32
黄昏前後…………………………… 46
好い手紙…………………………… 57
阿難と呪術師の娘………………… 61
鬼子母の愛………………………… 106

岡本かの子全集　2　小説　2
昭和49年6月30日

鶴は病みき………………………… 3
敵…………………………………… 35
渾沌未分…………………………… 54
決闘場……………………………… 79
春…………………………………… 95
明暗………………………………… 132
母子叙情…………………………… 142
川…………………………………… 254
高原の太陽………………………… 268
肉体の神曲………………………… 282
＊解題・校訂(近藤祐子)………… 397

岡本 かの子　おかもと・かのこ
現代短歌集　……現代日本文学全集38(改造)昭4
母子叙情　………新日本文学全集25(改造)昭15
巴里祭　…………新日本文学全集25(改造)昭15
やがて五月に　…新日本文学全集25(改造)昭15
夏の夜の夢　……新日本文学全集25(改造)昭15

Sample page of Gendai Nihon bungaku sōran shiriizu

publication of the collection. Series 2, *Zenshū sakkamei sōran* 全集作家名綜覧, is arranged by author. Under each author, the titles of his or her works appear, and each entry shows in what volume of which collection that entry appears and when it was published. The arrangement is by the date of publication. Series 3, *Zenshū sakuhinmei sōran* 全集作品名綜覧, arranged by the title of individual works, provides the author's name, where the work can be found, the publisher, and the date of publication. These three series cover literary works, including popular literature, criticism, chronologies, collected from 104 major literary collections in 3,200 volumes. *Sakuhinmei kara hikeru Nihon bungaku zenshū annai* 作品名から引ける日本文学全集案内 (X-7) is the same work published as *Gendai Nihon bungaku sōran shiriizu, 3: Zenshū sakuhinmei sōran*, although it does not say that anywhere in the book. The sections for chronology and criticism and the bibliography of authors from series 3 have been removed. Series 4, *Kojin zenshū naiyō sōran* 個人全集内容総覧, and 5, *Kojin zenshū sakuhinmei sōran* 個人全集作品名綜覧, function in the same way for 557 collections of 520 individual authors from the Meiji to the Shōwa eras. Series 4 lists the author in Japanese syllabary order and gives the publisher, numbers of volumes, dates, and, for each volume, the table of contents. Series 5 lists the titles of works. The authors that are cited include novelists, poets, essayists, critics, and philosophers.

Other convenient and much cheaper spinoffs of series 5 are *Sakuhinmei kara hikeru Nihon bungaku sakka, shōsetsuka, kojin zenshū annai* 作品名から引ける日本文学作家小説家個人全集案内 (X-8) and *Sakuhinmei kara hikeru Nihon bungaku hyōron, shisōka kojin zenshū annai* 作品名から引ける日本文学評論思想家個人全集案内 (X-9). *Nihon no shōsetsu zenjōhō 27/90* 日本の小説全情報 (X-10) is a list of 84,000 titles of novels and plays published between 1927 and 1990 by about 10,000 Japanese authors. Although the titles of complete works and selections of individual authors were included, titles of works that appeared in literary collections such as *bungaku zenshū*, titles of juvenile literature, and titles of translations of foreign literary works were not included. Titles are listed under an author's name in order of their date of publication and with complete bibliographic information. There is no title index, but there is a table of contents with author names in Japanese syllabary order. Since there is no access by title, this bibliography can only be used to supplement the one above.

For more recent literary works appearing, for example, in newspapers and literary journals, consult *Bungei nenkan* 文芸年鑑 (X-11) when you have fairly a good idea of the year of publication. This yearbook provides an overview of the previous year in the fields of literature (both domestic and foreign), theater, movies, broadcasting, publishing, art, music, and popular culture. A documents section lists all the literary works that appeared in over one hundred magazines and newspapers, literary awards, obituaries, movies, and directories.

While looking for information about books, you might have a problem reading some titles. Particularly difficult are the popular stories written during the Edo period and the titles of Kabuki plays. To help, there is *Nihon bungaku sakuhinmei yomikata jiten* 日本文学作品名よみかた辞典 (X-12). Although it is not the complete solution, it includes approximately 10,000 difficult-to-read titles selected from various literary genres. There is an index for Chinese characters with common readings, which can help you to decipher the proper readings of the titles.

Quiz X-1. Where can I find the text of *Fuseya no monogatari* ふせやの物語?

Quiz X-2. Where can I find *Musashi abumi* むさしあぶみ by Asai Ryōi 浅井了意?

Quiz X-3. Do you have *Kuroi ame* 黒い雨 by Ibuse Masuji 井伏鱒二 in any *zenshū*? I could not find it in the card or on-line catalogs.

Quiz X-4. Where can I find *Hato* 鳩 by Ōe Kenzaburō 大江健三郎?

2. INDEX TO POEMS AND PARTS OF *TANKA*

For individual *tanka* (*waka*) 短歌（和歌）of which you can only recall a phrase, use *Shinpen Kokka taikan* 新編国歌大観 (X-13). This completely revised edition added to its earlier edition thousands of poems from various sources, such as books of poetry contests (*utaawase*), stories, privately collected anthologies, and poetry collections (*chokusen wakashū*) edited by imperial command. In the

音訓よみガイド

き	清	193	**きん**	今	116	くすり	薬	330	**くん**	君	77
きょう	匡	65		近	71	くせ	曲	70		訓	77
	杏	65		欣	72	くだ	管	50		裙	77
	狂	65		金	72	くだく	摧	121		腥	78
	享	66		園	73	くち	口	102		薫	78
	京	66		童	73	くちる	朽	62	**ぐん**	軍	78
	況	67		琴	74	くつ	沓	252		群	78
	俠	67		釿	74		堀	76			
	狹	67		禁	74		厥	84	**【け】**		
	恐	67		禽	74	くつがえ					
	胸	68		檎	74	る	覆	299	け	化	27
	強	68		錦	74	くに	国	114		毛	326
	経	79	**ぎん**	吟	75	くぬぎ	橡	350		気	53
	教	68		銀	75	くばる	配	273		家	33
	梟	68				くび	首	147		華	34
	卿	68				くびかせ	鉗	87		袈	78

きん(琴, 釿, 禁, 禽, 檎, 錦)

【琴】

琴歌譜　きんかふ
　　歌謡集・成立年未詳　編者未詳
琴所稿剛　きんしょこうさん
　　江戸中期の漢詩文集　沢村琴所
琴声美人伝　きんせいびじんでん
　　江戸後期の草双紙　山東京伝
琴後集　ことじりしゅう
　　和歌和文集・成立年未詳　村田春海
琴腹　ことはら
　　御伽草子・成立年未詳　作者未詳

【釿】

釿始　ちょうなはじめ
　　江戸中期の俳諧集　助叟編

【禁】

禁腋秘抄　きんえきひしょう
　　有職故実・成立年未詳　著者未詳

　　昭和期の小説　川端康成

【檎】

檎　あさがお
　　昭和期の長編小説　古井由吉
檎城抄　きんいきしょう
　　昭和期の評論　阿倍能成
檎花戯書　はちすざれがき
　　昭和期の詩集　城昌幸

【錦】

錦江稿本　きんこうこうほん
　　叢書・成立年未詳　馬場錦江
錦繡　きんしゅう
　　昭和期の長編小説　宮本輝
錦繡段　きんしゅうだん
　　室町中期の漢詩集　天隠竜沢編
錦城茶話　きんじょうさわ
　　随筆・成立年未詳　大田元貞
錦所談　きんしょだん
　　江戸後期の随筆　山田以文述
錦西随筆　きんせいずいひつ

Sample page of Nihon bungaku sakuhinmei yomikata jiten

―たちともみえぬ
―なかむるそらも
―ふみみしあとに
―ゆくもかへるも
きりたちて
きりたちて
きりたちて
きりたちぬなり
きりたちのほる

20 新後拾 三六四
9 新勅撰 二七五
9 新勅撰 一二九一
21 新続古 五四五
1 古今 二五一
8 新古今 一六九四
21 新続古 五九三
16 続後拾 三一五
8 新古今 四九一

きりにしつめる
きりにしをるる
きりになほ
きりにのこれる
きりのあなたに
きりのあなたに
きりのあなたに
きりのいとにも
きりのいろより

14 玉葉 七四七
8 新古今 四九二
15 続千載 九三一
12 続拾遺 三三六
14 玉葉 五六八
14 玉葉 二〇五三
17 風雅 五五五
19 新拾遺 一八八一
17 風雅 五一七

四七三 新古今和歌集巻第五秋歌下〔8 新古今〕

四五〇

四七三 しのねも長きよあかぬ古郷に猶おもひそふ松かぜぞふく
　　　百首歌中に
　　　　　　　　　　　　　　　　　　　　　　式子内親王

四七四 あともなき庭のあさぢにむすぼれ露のそこなる松虫の声
　　　題しらず
　　　　　　　　　　　　　　　　　　　　　　藤原輔尹朝臣

四七五 秋風は身にしむばかり吹きにけりいまやうつらむいもがさごろも
　　　　　　　　　　　　　　　　　　　　　　前大僧正慈円

四七六 衣うつおとは枕にすがはらや伏見の夢をいくよのこしつ
　　　和歌所歌合に、秋歌
　　　　　　　　　　　　　　　　　　　　　　権中納言公経

四七七 衣うつねやまのいほのしばしばもしらぬゆめぢにむすぶ手枕
　　　千五百番歌合に、秋歌
　　　　　　　　　　　　　　　　　　　　　　摂政太政大臣

四九〇 秋の夜ははやながら月に成りにけりことわりなりやねざめせらる
　　　五十首歌たてまつりし時
　　　　　　　　　　　　　　　　　　　　　　寂蓮法師

四九一 むらさめのつゆもまだひぬ槙のはに霧立ちのぼる秋の夕ぐれ
　　　秋歌とて
　　　　　　　　　　　　　　　　　　　　　　太上天皇

四九二 さびしさは深山の秋のあさぐもり霧にしをるる槙の下露
　　　河霧といふこと
　　　　　　　　　　　　　　　　　　　　　　左衛門督通光

四九三 あけぼのや河せの浪のたかせぶねくだすか人の袖の秋ぎり
　　　堀河院御時、百首歌たてまつりけるに、霧をよめる
　　　　　　　　　　　　　　　　　　　　　　権大納言公実

四九四 ふもとをば宇治の川霧たちこめて雲井にみゆるあさ日山かな

Sample page of Shinpen Kokka taikan

revised edition the scope of the old *Kokka taikan* (about 170 sources indexed) has been greatly enlarged, with over 800 new sources, although the indexing system remains basically the same. Entries are numbered (numbers from the old edition were carried over), and this number is an important identification tool for quotation among researchers in the field. It can also be used for finding the text of a collection of poetry by either author or title.

Shiika zenshū, series 6-8 of *Gendai Nihon bungaku sōran shiriizu* (X-6), encompasses thirty-five poetry (modern style, *tanka*, and *haiku*) collections in 426 volumes from 1929 to 1984. It can be used to locate modern poetry. Series 6, *Shiika zenshū shiika naiyō sōran* 詩歌全集詩歌内容綜覧, is the table of contents index and lists the contents of the poetry collections. Series 7, *Shiika zenshū sakkamei sōran* 詩歌全集作家名綜覧, is the author index and lists the names of the poets in the collections. Series 8, *Shiika zenshū sakuhinmei sōran* 詩歌全集作品名綜覧, is the title index and lists the titles of poems.

Another convenient index to locate poems included in poetry collections of individual poets is *Sakuhinmei kara hikeru Nihon bungaku shiika, haijin kojin zenshū annai* 作品名から引ける日本文学詩歌俳人個人全集案内 (X-14). This index contains the titles or first lines of over 87,000 poems that appeared in 115 poetry collections of 112 Japanese poets of the modern period published by the year 1984. *Nihon no shiika zenjōhō 27/90* 日本の詩歌全情報 (X-15) lists the titles and bibliographic data for approximately 40,000 poetry collections (modern poetry, *waka/tanka*, *haiku*, and *senryu*) written by 23,000 Japanese poets since 1868 and published between 1927 and 1990. An individual poet's collections, selections, and anthologies were included; collections of poems by several poets do not appear. This reference work can give you information about individual collections, but not about individual poems.

Quiz X-5. I am trying to remember the first word of a *waka/tanka* of which I can remember only the last two phrases. They are *Izuko mo onaji aki no yūgure* いずこも同じ秋の夕暮.

Quiz X-6. I am looking for a poem titled *Ubaguruma* 乳母車 by Miyoshi Tatsuji 三好達治.

Quiz X-7. I am looking for a collection of *waka* by Michitsuna no Haha 道綱母 , the author of *Kagerō nikki* 蜻蛉日記.

3. TRANSLATIONS

Meiji Taishō Shōwa hon'yaku bungaku mokuroku 明治大正昭和翻訳文学目録 (X-16) is explained best by its added English title, *A List of Foreign Literary Works Translated into Japanese*. This covers translations made from 1868 to 1955 of Western novels, dramas, poems, essays, diaries, or letters. The major portion covers the Taishō period and after, 1912 to 1955. This portion is arranged in Japanese syllabary order of the author's name followed by the original spelling and nationality. Translations that appeared in journals are not included. The second part is arranged by chronological order. Entries are arranged by title and include the author (when known), the author's nationality (when known), the translator, and the publisher or the name of the journal or newspaper. This portion does not include original titles. An author index for part 1 is included.

Hon'yaku tosho mokuroku 翻訳図書目録 is a bibliography of Japanese translations since 1977 of foreign books on all subjects. It should be used if you need to find a recent translation of foreign literature into Japanese since there is no reference work devoted solely to translations of recent foreign literature. The arrangement is by alphabetical order and Japanese syllabary order in *kana*. There are indexes of original titles, translation titles, and authors.

To find out which Japanese literary works have been translated into Western languages, consult *Japanese Literature in European Languages: A Bibliography* (X-17), *Modern Japanese Literature in Translation: A Bibliography* (X-18), and *Japanese Literature in Foreign Languages 1945–1990* (X-19). The first was compiled by the Japan P.E.N. Club as a checklist of writings on Japanese literature for the occasion of the 29th International Congress of P.E.N. in 1957. The second edition includes works written in or translated into European languages and published by the end of 1960. It includes both books and periodical articles and can also be used as a bibliography of materials relative to Japanese literature. It is divided into five sections: (1) General, (2) Classical, (3) Classical Theater, (4) Modern Literature, and (5) Juvenile and Folk Literature. The section for modern literature is subdivided into novels and short stories, poetry and drama, and essays and biographies.

Modern Japanese Literature in Translation was compiled by the International House of Japan and covers materials published from 1868 through 1977. This is an enlarged and revised edition of *Modern Japanese Literature in Western Translations: A Bibliography*. It includes translations of modern Japanese literary works that appeared in periodicals as well, and the scope was widened to include works from other Asian languages. It also covers the translations of modern Japanese literary works, primarily fiction, drama, poetry and essays, and literary criticism, published since 1867. It is arranged in alphabetical order by the romanized reading of the author's name, followed by Japanese writing, with dates. The compiler says that this bibliography excludes studies of the literature of other countries, but some literary essays in that category are included. It has indexes of translators and titles. Entries are arranged in alphabetical order under each author, and information varies depending on the type of work. Works of fiction are arranged in alphabetical order, followed by the title of the translation, the translator's name, place of publication, publisher, date of publication, and number of pages. Essays, poems, and other works are entered as "E," or "P," or "*tanka,*" or "*haiku,*" and so forth rather than as individual works, and they are arranged chronologically by date of publication. *Japanese Literature in Foreign Languages 1945-1990* includes translations of Japanese books, articles, and dissertations into Western languages during the years from 1945 to 1990. (A volume for oriental languages will be published separately.) It is arranged alphabetically by the name of the author, and approximately 15,000 items by 4,138 authors are included. Each author, or title if the work is anonymous, appears in romanized form and then in Japanese, followed by dates, and, under each author by alphabetical order of the title, with an indication of the language of the translation. A general index is at the end of the volume.

Quiz X-8. I want to find Japanese translations of *Gulliver's Travels* by Jonathan Swift. Is there more than one translation available?

Quiz X-9. I would like to read the original of *Master of Go* by Kawabata Yasunari 川端康成.

Quiz X-10. Which work of Mishima Yukio was translated into the most foreign languages?

4. HISTORY OF JAPANESE LITERATURE

For studying and understanding the history of Japanese literature in general, *Nihon bungaku zenshi* 日本文学全史 (X-20) has a unique viewpoint. It gives a general description of the history of Japan and explains the history of literature in the context of this broader history.

Nihon bungaku dainenpyō (IX-13) is a chronology of literary works and people, including drama, art, literary criticism, foreign literature, and journals, covering the period from ancient times to 1985.

5. DICTIONARIES AND ENCYCLOPEDIAS FOR JAPANESE LITERATURE

The primary encyclopedic dictionary in this field is *Nihon bungaku daijiten* 日本文学大辞典 (X-21), compiled by Fujimura Tsukuru. It covers Japanese literature, language, art, drama, mythology, foreign literature, Japanese traditional music, Buddhism, Shinto, and other topics from the ancient times to the end of Taishō era (1925). Scholarly and evaluative articles were written by specialists in their respective fields. Explanations are detailed, and entries include bibliographical references arranged in Japanese syllabary order and illustrations. Each entry includes the reading and subject area. Coverage was extended to the early part of the Shōwa era by the supplementary volume, but this information was not incorporated into the main volumes. The supplementary volume consists of a supplement to the text of first edition, a chronological table to 1950, a general index, and an index of hard-to-read Chinese characters. It is well illustrated in black and white. To replace or supplement part of this aging encyclopedia, *Nihon koten bungaku daijiten* 日本古典文学大辞典 (X-22) was published. This is a comprehensive encyclopedic dictionary of Japanese classical literature that includes 13,000 entries (9,200 titles of books, 2,600 personal names, and 1,200 other items) by

857 contributors. It has many interdisciplinary entries for such areas as Japanese linguistics, Chinese classics, religious texts, arts, calligraphy and painting, and gazetteers to the end of the Edo period (1868). Cross-referencing is well done, and bibliographies include well-selected basic works. The obvious difference between this and *Nihon bungaku daijiten* is the inclusion of the latest scholarship. Volume 6 contains a general index and a list of readings for hard-to-read words.

Nihon Kindai Bungaku daijiten 日本近代文学大事典 (X-23) is an encyclopedic dictionary of modern Japanese literature. It has an extensive coverage of popular literature, children's literature, and essays and includes information from specialists on Japanese literature and related fields such as philosophy, movies, dramas, newspapers, illustrators, and publishing. It is particularly good for post-Meiji literature. Articles are signed and include references. The first three volumes cover people, volume 4 covers general entries, volume 5 covers newspapers and journals, and volume 6 covers monographic series and literary collections and includes an index. Literary authors and scholars of the Edo period who were alive until the early Meiji era are also discussed.

The following two biographical dictionaries are also useful to start your research: *Biographical Dictionary of Japanese Literature* compiled by Hisamatsu Sen'ichi (Tokyo: International Society for Educational Information, 1976; 437p.) and *Biographical Dictionary of Japanese History* edited by Iwao Seiichi and translated by Burton Watson (Tokyo: Kodansha International in collaboration with the International Society for Educational Information, 1978. 655 p.)

Although some dictionaries and encyclopedias of Japanese literature include miscellaneous information in appendixes or tables, books such as *The Princeton Companion to Classical Japanese Literature* (X-24) have become very handy for students and scholars of Japanese classical literature, particularly those who speak English. It includes essays on literary history, authors, and important works in dictionary format along with chronological tables. It is a very useful reference work loaded with information on Japanese literature and culture.

Quiz X-11. When did Tsubouchi Shōyō 坪内逍遥 translate Walter Scott's *Bride of Lammermoor* as *Shunpū jōwa* 春風情話?

128   CHAPTER TEN

Quiz X-12. Where can I find studies and commentaries on the major works of Hotta Yoshie 堀田善衛?

Quiz X-13. I want information on *Sarashina nikki* 更科日記 and its author.

Quiz X-14. I need to find a commentary on *Goshūi wakashū* 後拾遺和歌集.

6. HISTORY OF THE STUDY OF JAPANESE LITERATURE

The most important collection is *Zōho kokugo kokubungaku kenkyūshi taisei* 増補国語国文学研究史大成 (X-25), originally published in 1960–61 and enlarged in 1977. The text of most of the earlier volumes is unchanged, and only the bibliographic sections were enlarged, and they were added at the end rather than incorporated into the text. The collection includes information on both books and journals. The main part consists of bibliographic essays, and each section contains an overview, a discussion of future research, and an annotated bibliography. There are various appendixes and an index, but these do not deal with the enlarged section.

For the most recent information, check the annual review of the field of Japanese literature that appears in major journals such as *Kokugo to kokubungaku kaishaku to kanshō* and *Bungaku gogaku*.

7. BIBLIOGRAPHIES OF RESEARCH MATERIALS

The standard bibliographies of Japanese literature are generally excellent source materials, although their coverage of journal articles is weak. The following six bibliographies of Japanese literature are standard. *Kokugo kokubun kenkyū zasshi sakuin* 国語国文学研究雑誌索引 (X-26), which originally appeared as supplements to no. 37 of *Kokugo kokubun no kenkyū*, covers the years from 1868 to 1931. *Kokugo kokubungaku nenkan* 国語国文学年鑑 (X-27), compiled by Hisamatsu Sen'ichi in three volumes, covers the period from 1938 to 1940. Although this yearbook stopped publication after the third issue, it established the pattern for later works. It was intended to include everything that had happened during the year in the fields of Japanese language and literature. It is divided into five sections: overview, index to journal articles, articles from newspapers, an annotated list of books, and various types of information and news. It also includes an author index. *Kokubungaku kenkyū bunken mokuroku: Shōwa 16-nen-Shōwa 37-nen* 国文学研究文献目録：昭和１６年 - 昭和３７年 (X-28), compiled by Kokubungaku Kenkyū Shiryōkan, covers the years from 1941 to 1962. This was prepared based on journals held at Kokubungaku Kenkyū Shiryōkan, and its coverage was meant to fill the gap between Hisamatsu's yearbooks and *Kokugo kokubungaku kenkyū bunken mokuroku, 1963–1970* 国語国文学研究文献目録 (X-29). It classified 36,000 articles, which appeared in approximately 480 *kiyō* 紀要 and other journals, into eight areas: Japanese literature in general, *jōdai* 上代, *chūko* 中古, *chūsei* 中世, *kinsei* 近世, *kindai* 近代, Japanese language, and the teaching of these fields. Under each classification, entries are subdivided into several sections. In addition to the separate Japanese language section, each major section has its own subdivision for Japanese language. Its appendix lists the journals indexed. *Kokugo kokubungaku kenkyū bunken mokuroku*, which covers the period from 1963 to 1970, includes both books and journal articles on Japanese language and literature published during the year. *Kokubungaku kenkyū bunken mokuroku* 国文学研究文献目録 (X-30) is a continuation of the above and covers the same subject matter for the years 1971 to 1976. *Kokubungaku nenkan* 国文学年鑑 (X-31), a further continuation, is the standard annual bibliography of Japanese literature and a yearbook for various other information in the field.

Besides these six standard bibliographies in the field of Japanese literature, there are many other supplemental ones. *Nihon bungaku kenkyū bunken yōran* 日本文学研究文献要覧 (X-32), which covers the years 1965 to 1976, and *Zasshi kiji sakuin: Jinbun, shakai hen. Ruiseki sakuinban: Bungaku hen* (II-2) are two examples. For the time between 1932 and 1937, there is no systematic periodical index for Japanese literature, and you thus have to check old issues of journals such as *Kokugo kokubun* 国語国文. As we have suggested before, for the most recent research and publications, check major scholastic journals in the field of Japanese literature, such as *Bungaku gogaku* and *Nihon bungaku*.

Quiz X-15. I need to find articles about Hayashi Fumiko 林芙美子 that were published before 1945.

Quiz X-16. I am looking for journal articles written after her death about Enchi Fumiko 円地文子 and her work.

8. INFORMATION ON INDIVIDUAL AUTHORS

There are numerous bibliographies on individual authors, and we cannot possibly include all of them here. Check handbooks such as *Nihon no sankō tosho: Kaisetsu sōran* (V-3) and *Gendai bungaku kenkyū: Jōhō to shiryō* 現代文学研究：情報と資料 (X-33), for example. The latter includes information on approximately three hundred modern literary authors.

Based on *Kindai sakka kenkyū jiten,* which was published in 1983, *Meiji Taishō Shōwa sakka kenkyū daijiten* 明治大正昭和作家研究大辞典 (X-34) includes information on 260 well-known modern novelists, poets, literary critics, and authors of juvenile literature. Each entry has a brief biography of the author, the current status of research and suggestions for future research on the author, and a bibliography of books and articles. *Nihon bungaku kenkyū shiryō sōsho* 日本文学研究資料叢書 is also a very useful guide to modern authors and their works.

If you do not have enough time to collect and read all of the materials available on your topic by bibliographic search, you need to sift the information you have collected by using a selective bibliography such as *Kokubungaku kenkyū shomoku kaidai* 国文学研究書目解題 edited by Ichiko Teiji, which only lists carefully selected major research works. You also need to learn the skill of sifting for the important and relevant materials for your research by, for instance, checking the bibliography of a standard history of Japanese literature and a history of the study of Japanese literature. Often you can also find well-selected, important materials in the reference section of dictionaries or encyclopedias in the field. Another good source for determining basic works is a handbook, manual, or introduction to the field of Japanese literature. Journal articles that provide an overview of recent trends in the field often have a selective bibliography of recent important studies. The books and articles listed in the bibliography section of *Nihon bungaku kenkyū shiryō sōsho* 日本文学研究資料叢書 (X-35) can also help, and *Kōza Nihon bungaku* 講座日本文学 (X-36) is another valuable research tool. Finally, talk to your professor about where to turn to find the basic and the latest information on your topic.

Information on criticism, chronology, and trends in research about individual authors can often be found in the individual author's collected works (*kojin zenshū* 個人全集), special issues (*tokushū-gō* 特集号) of major journals in Japanese literature, and handbooks for literary studies (*bungaku kenkyū hikkei* 文学研究必携) in a very convenient and condensed form.

Quiz X-17. On what topic did Mishima Yukio 三島由紀夫 lecture in Ann Arbor? When was it?

Quiz X-18. What is the current status of research about Dazai Osamu 太宰治 ?

9. ACQUIRING MATERIALS FOUND THROUGH BIBLIOGRAPHIC SEARCH

Now that you have a list of selected bibliographies you would like to read, you need to find these books and articles so that you can examine them. The *National Union Catalog*, on-line catalogs such as RLIN-CJK and OCLC-CJK, printed catalogs of individual libraries of the major East Asian collections, and your own library's catalog are some of the sources. The *Union List of Serials, New Serial Titles, Japanese Periodicals and Newspapers in Western Languages* and the *National Union List of Current Japanese Serials in East Asian Libraries of North America* (IV-5) (see chapter four) are major sources of journal holdings, mainly in the United States and Canada. Before you think about going to Japan for research or request copies of journal articles from Japanese libraries, exhaust the sources available within this country.

Kokubungaku Kenkyū Shiryōkanzō chikuji kankōbutsu mokuroku 国文学研究資料館蔵逐次刊行物目録 (X-37) divides 1,332 scholastic journals on Japanese literature into three groups: (1) those titles that begin with Chinese characters or *kana*, arranged in Japanese syllabary order; (2) those titles that begin with the romanized form arranged in alphabetical order; and (3) Western-language journals arranged in alphabetical order. Information pertaining to title changes, mergers, and suspension or cessation of publication is included. *Nihon Kindai Bungakukan shozō shuyō zasshi mokuroku* 日本近代文学館所蔵主要雑誌目録 (X-38) is also useful for locating journal articles in Japan in the field of Japanese literature, in addition to the general periodical holding lists such as *Kokuritsu Kokkai Toshokan shozō kokunai chikuji kankōbutsu mokuroku* (IV-5) or *Gakujutsu zasshi sōgō mokuroku: Wabun hen* (IV-6).

Another important source for journal articles, particularly *kiyō* 紀要,[1] which are often not available in the United States, is *Kokubungaku nenjibetsu ronbunshū* 国文学年次別論文集 (X-39). This is a very valuable source of scholastic journal articles collected from various *kiyō* and annals of societies in the field of Japanese literature. Published since 1980, it is reprinted annually, and each year it is divided into six sections: general, *jōdai* 上代, *chūko* 中古, *chūsei* 中世, *kinsei* 近世, and *kindai* 近代. It does not include monthly journals. For other sources of articles and books that were not included in this collection, a list in the form of a table of contents is appended at the end of each field.

IMPORTANT REFERENCE BOOKS DISCUSSED IN THIS CHAPTER

X-1. Kokuritsu Kokkai Toshokan. *Zenshū sōsho saimoku sōran: Koten hen.* Tokyo: Kinokuniya Shoten, 1977–89. 3v.

X-2. Hirose Toshi, comp. *Nihon sōsho sakuin*, new ed. Tokyo: Meicho Kankōkai, 1969. 1v.

X-3. Hanawa Hokinoichi. *Gunsho ruijū.* Tokyo: Naigai Shoseki, 1928–31. 39v. Reprint by Gunsho Ruijū Kanseikai, 1959–60. 29v.

_____. *Zoku Gunsho ruijū.* Tokyo: Zoku Gunsho Ruijū Kankōkai, 1931–33. 84v.

1. *Kiyō* is an esoteric term that covers serial publications, particularly those periodicals published under the names of research institutes and other learned societies, such as departments of universities, which publish research reports by their members. These research bodies usually are not directly responsible for the contents of the articles.

_____. *Zoku Zoku Gunsho ruijū*. Tokyo: Kokusho Kanseikai, 1906–9. 22v. Reprint by Zoku Gunsho Ruijū Kankōkai, 1970. 16v.

_____. *Gunsho kaidai*. Tokyo: Gunsho Ruijū Kankōkai, 1960–67. 31v. in 23v.

X-4. *Nihon zuihitsu taisei*. Tokyo: Yoshikawa Kōbunkan, 1973–83. 59v.
    Nihon zuihitsu taisei, 1-ki. 23v.
    Nihon zuihitsu taisei, 2-ki. 24v.
    Zoku Nihon zuihitsu taisei, bekkan. 12v.

X-5. Ōta Tamesaburō. *Nihon zuihitsu sakuin*. Reprint. Tokyo: Iwanami Shoten, 1963. 2v.

X-6. *Gendai Nihon bungaku sōran shiriizu*. Tokyo: Nichigai Asoshieitsu, 1982–.

X-7. *Sakuhinmei kara hikeru Nihon bungaku zenshū annai*. Tokyo: Nichigai Asoshieitsu, 1984. 838p.

X-8. *Sakuhinmei kara hikeru Nihon bungaku sakka, shōsetsuka kojin zenshū annai*. Tokyo: Nichigai Asoshieitsu, 1992. 15, 1,027p.

X-9. *Sakuhinmei kara hikeru Nihon bungaku hyōron, shisōka kojin zenshū annai*. Tokyo: Nichigai Asoshieitsu, 1992.

X-10. *Nihon no shōsetsu zenjōhō 27/90*. Tokyo: Nichigai Asoshieitsu, 1991. 2v.

X-11. Nihon Bungeika Kyōkai, comp. *Bungei nenkan*. Tokyo: Shinchōsha, 1929–.

X-12. *Nihon bungaku sakuhinmei yomikata jiten*. Tokyo: Nichigai Asoshieitsu, 1988. 35, 444p.

X-13. Shinpen Kokka Taikan Henshū Iinkai. *Shinpen Kokka taikan*. Tokyo: Kadokawa Shoten, 1983–87. 10v.

X-14. *Sakuhinmei kara hikeru Nihon bungaku shiika, haijin kojin zenshū annai*. Tokyo: Nichigai Asoshieitsu, 1992.

X-15. *Nihon no shiika zenjōhō 27/90*. Tokyo: Nichigai Asoshieitsu, 1992. 160, 1,309p.

X-16. Kokuritsu Kokkai Toshokan. *Meiji Taishō Shōwa hon'yaku bungaku mokuroku*. Tokyo: Kazama Shobō, 1959. 779p.

X-17. Japan P.E.N. Club, comp. *Japanese Literature in European Languages: A Bibliography*, 2d ed. Tokyo: The Club, 1961. xii, 98p.

X-18. Kokusai Bunka Kaikan. Toshoshitsu. *Modern Japanese Literature in Translation: A Bibliography*. Tokyo and New York: Kodansha International, 1979. 311p.

X-19. Japan P.E.N. Club, comp. *Japanese Literature in Foreign Languages 1945–1990*. Tokyo: Japan Book Publishers Association, 1990. 5, 383p.

X-20. Ichiko Teiji. *Nihon bungaku zenshi*, enl. ed. Tokyo: Gakutōsha, 1990. 6v.

X-21. Fujimura Tsukuru, comp. *Nihon bungaku daijiten,* new, rev. and enl. ed. Tokyo: Shinchōsha, 1950–52. 7v.

X-22. *Nihon koten bungaku daijiten*. Tokyo: Iwanami Shoten, 1983–85. 6v.

X-23. Nihon Kindai Bungakukan. *Nihon Kindai Bungaku daijiten*. Tokyo: Kōdansha, 1977–78. 6v.

X-24. Miner, Earl, Hiroko Odagiri, and Robert E. Morrell. *The Princeton Companion to Classical Japanese Literature*. Princeton, NJ: Princeton University Press, 1985. xxi, 570p.

X-25. *Zōho kokugo kokubungaku kenkyūshi taisei*. Tokyo: Sanseidō, 1977–78. 15v.

X-26. Naniwa Kōtō Gakkō. *Kokugo kokubun kenkyū zasshi sakuin*. Bound ed. Kyoto: Hoshino Shoten, 1933. 424, 582, 210, 38p.

X-27. Hisamatsu Sen'ichi. *Kokugo kokubungaku nenkan*. Tokyo: Seibunsha, 1938–40. 3v.

X-28. *Kokubungaku kenkyū bunken mokuroku: Shōwa 16-nen-Shōwa 37-nen*. Tokyo: Kokubungaku Kenkyū Shiryōkan, 1984. 11, 748, 85, 9p.

X-29. Tōkyō Daigaku Kokugo Kokubun Gakkai, comp. *Kokugo kokubungaku kenkyū bunken mokuroku, 1963–1970*. Tokyo: Shibundō, 1965–72.

X-30. Kokubungaku Kenkyū Shiryōkan, comp. *Kokubungaku kenkyū bunken mokuroku*. Tokyo: Kokubungaku Kenkyū Shiryōkan, 1971–76.

X-31. Kokubungaku Kenkyū Shiryōkan, comp. *Kokubungaku nenkan*. Tokyo: Shibundō, 1979–.

X-32. *Nihon bungaku kenkyū bunken yōran*. Tokyo: Nichigai Asoshieitsu, 1976–77. 3v.

X-33. Hasegawa Izumi et al. *Gendai bungaku kenkyū: Jōhō to shiryō*. Tokyo: Shibundō, 1987. 588p.

X-34. *Meiji Taishō Shōwa sakka kenkyū daijiten*. Tokyo: Ōfūsha, 1992. 619p.

X-35. *Nihon bungaku kenkyū shiryō sōsho*. Tokyo: Yūseidō, 1969–.

X-36. *Kōza Nihon bungaku*. Tokyo: Sanseidō, 1968–71.

X-37. *Kokubungaku Kenkyū Shiryōkanzō chikuji kankōbutsu mokuroku*. Tokyo: Kokubungaku Kenkyū Shiryōkan, 1977–.

X-38. *Nihon Kindai Bungakukan shozō shuyō zasshi mokuroku*. Tokyo: Nihon Kindai Bungakukan, 1981–.

X-39. Gakujutsu Bunken Kankōkai. *Kokubungaku nenjibetsu ronbunshū*. Tokyo: Hōbun Shuppan, 1980–.

Chapter Eleven
Technicalities of Style

It is important to familiarize yourself with the style manual that your instructor requires for your report. There are a few well-known tools that provide consistent styles and formats for typography, spelling, capitalization, punctuation, footnotes, and bibliographies. *The Chicago Manual of Style,* published by the University of Chicago Press, frequently revised and designed to offer standards for scholarly writing, is the most detailed manual of this type and probably the most frequently used among academics and professional editors. Other manuals of style include the *MLA Handbook for Writers of Research Papers* and *Modern Researcher. Turabian's Manual for Writers of Term Papers, Theses, and Dissertations* is a much smaller manual that gives examples of different types of problems encountered in composing footnotes and bibliographies.

When typing your manuscript for publication in scholarly journals, check recent issues of the target journal for format and style of references, bibliographic footnotes, and other features. Often scholarly journals specify which format to follow. For instance, the *Journal of Asian Studies,* along with its own specifications, urges authors to consult and follow the format for footnotes in *The Chicago Manual of Style.* But because of the problems unique to the Japanese language, you might have to deviate from the standard guidelines found in style manuals when writing names. For instance, instead of reversing the name order, Japanese names that appear in scholarly journals and books are given family name first, followed by the first name, as we have done throughout this book. When in doubt, follow the current practice in your field. Whichever manual you use, the most important thing is to be consistent and accurate. Uniformity of format and accuracy are very important. Herschel Webb, in *Research in Japanese Sources: A Guide* (pp. 127–34), discusses many aspects and problems of compiling bibliographies in the field of Japanese studies. If you don't know which style to follow, pick one and be consistent. This will make it easier to correct later since correcting an inaccurate entry is not as time-consuming as restoring uniformity among the entries as a whole.

If you are compiling an annotated bibliography, clearly state the scope of your bibliography: coverage of topics, duration of date of publication, and types of materials included or excluded. Select the items that you want to include in each entry. Author, co-author, translator if applicable, title, series title, numbering in the series if there is one, date and place of publication, publisher, and numbers of volumes or pages are usually the minimum information to be included for books. When the spine, the cover, the title page, and the colophon have different titles, the title on the title page is generally taken as the formal title. In the case of paperback books, the title on the cover is often considered the formal title. But sometimes in Japanese books only the title on the colophon is the real title. The date of publication is sometimes not easy to determine, particularly in the case of old publications. Many Japanese publishers use the term *han* 版 , "edition," to indicate a printing, and whether the book is really an edition or merely a printing can be determined by the time lapse from the original date of publication, by the numbers shown as editions, by the preface or the afterword, or by the copyright date. For old works, the preface date sometimes is the only date in the book. In other cases, because of the modesty of Japanese publishers, the last publisher listed in the colophon is often the most important one. Many modern publishers include the words *Kabushiki Gaisha*, meaning company. Most of these are omitted from bibliographic information as long as the abbreviated names are identifiable. Sometimes, the physical number of volumes does not match the actual number of volumes in a bibliographic unit, *kan* or *maki* 巻. In these cases, the number of volumes is recorded as ten volumes in five.

For journal articles, you need to include author, title of the article, journal title, volume and number of the journal, date of issue, and page numbers.

There is more than one system of romanization of the Japanese language. It differs depending on the field, but normally in the United States, particularly in libraries, the Hepburn system is used. *Kenkyusha's New Japanese-English Dictionary* is closely based on this system, and thus consult this standard dictionary when in doubt. It has a table of romanization that includes other systems such as *kunrei-shiki* ("the official system") and *Nihon-shiki* ("the Japan system"), which are used mostly in Japan. Additional ways of romanization deviating from these standard ones are also in use. Words such as Suematz, Satow, and Itoh are based on their pronunciation in Western languages. Another kind of romanization was influenced by the historical *kanazukai* (*kana* usage) seen in words such as Kwannon, Kwantō, Yedo, Uyematsu, and Inouye.[1]

Two diacritical marks are used, the apostrophe and the macron. The apostrophe is used to show that the adjoining two letters are pronounced separately, as in the case of Ken'ichi [ken-i-ti], not [keni-ti]. The macron, which is used for long vowels, is often omitted in English texts.

Japanese is an agglutinative language, and it is rather difficult to set clear rules for word division. Particles are treated as separate words, but what about compound words such as *Nihongo* and *Nihonshi*? The Library of Congress considers *Nihongo* as one word but separates *Nihon shi* into two words. The Library of Congress's rules in romanizing Japanese words, although they often seem arbitrary, became necessary because of the use of on-line computer searches. When performing an on-line search, try different ways of dividing words until you are successful. When writing a paper, check the style sheet of the journal or publisher. Rules for the romanization of Japanese words appeared in *Library of Congress Cataloging Service Bulletin* 20 (Spring 1983), pp. 51-65.

SAMPLE BIBLIOGRAPHIC ENTRY FOR BOOKS

Kuroita Katsumi and Maruyama Jirō. *Kokushi taikei.* 66 vols. Tokyo: Yoshikawa Kōbunkan, 1929–64.

Kobayashi Zenhachi. *Nihon shuppan bunkashi.* Nihon Shoshigaku Taikei 1. Tokyo: Seishodō, 1978.

---

1. For details of *kanazukai*, refer to the *Kodansha Encyclopedia of Japan* (VII-29) under *kana*.

SAMPLE BIBLIOGRAPHIC ENTRY FOR JOURNAL ARTICLES

Igarashi Takeshi. "Nichi-Bei kōzō kyōgi no imi to wa nani ka." *Gaikō Forum* 3.4 (April 1990): 14-23.

When headings of the title catalog, for example, are arranged in *kana* syllabary order, not by romanized form, you need to know some basic filing rules as follows:

1. *Kutōten* 句読点 ("punctuation marks") are ignored.
2. *Dakuon* 濁音 ("voiced sound") and *handakuon* 半濁音 ("p-sound") are arranged as *seion* 清音 ("voiceless sound"), for example, バ, パ, - - - ハ.
3. Small letters of *yōon* 拗音 ("contracted sound") and *sokuon* 促音 ("double consonant") and in words of foreign origin are handled as *seion* 正音 (each *kana* is read as if it is independent of the others), for example, きょういく - - - きよういく, はっけん - - - はつけん, ジェット - - - ジエット.
4. Alphabetizing is letter by letter, with word separations ignored, for example, わせだいがくし = わせだ だいがくし - - - わせたたいかくし.
5. For romanized headings it is common to ignore macrons, so Kyūshū 九州 = Kyushu.

For other types of problems you will encounter during a bibliographic search, such as the handling of vestigial prefix terms of titles, two-line subtitles, the arrangement of corporate author names, multiple or discontinuous pagination sequences, and volume designations, refer to the Nippon Cataloging Rules (NCR)[2] or consult your instructor or librarian.

---

2. Nihon Toshokan Kyōkai Mokuroku Iinkai, ed., *Nihon mokuroku kisoku* [Nippon cataloging rules] (Tokyo: Nihon Toshokan Kyōkai, 1987).

Chapter Twelve
Japanese Libraries and Research Institutions

Japanese libraries, particularly college and university libraries, are very different from those in the United States. Before you go to Japan to do research, find out, if possible, which libraries have the materials you will need by consulting library book catalogs or the other bibliographic tools we have already mentioned in this guide, such as *Kokusho sōmokuroku* (I-16), *Kokuritsu Kokkai Toshokan zōsho mokuroku* (I-21), and *Gakujutsu zasshi sōgō mokuroku: Wabun hen* (IV-6). The national network for academic libraries, Gakujutsu Jōhō Sentaa (NACSIS), has a comprehensive database of academic journals, but there is nothing for books that corresponds to the *National Union Catalog* here in the United States. A wide variety of directories of special libraries, museums, and research institutions may be consulted. For literature, for example, there are special libraries such as Kokubungaku Kenkyū Shiryōkan and Nihon Kindai Bungakukan and other special collections scattered throughout Japan.

Contact the Japanese libraries you intend to use before you leave the United States and find out what you need to do to use their collections. Japanese libraries are much more restrictive than those in the United States. Often they require a letter of introduction from your university librarian, your professor, or the chairman of your department. Also, seek information about Japanese libraries that have strong collections in your field from your professors and colleagues or through various reference tools in your library, such as *Zenkoku tokushu korekushon yōran* 全国特殊コレクション要覧, 2d ed. (Tokyo: Shuppan Nyūsusha, 1977), which lists 2,300 special collections of 700 institutions, *Senmon jōhō kikan sōran* 専門情報機関総覧 (Directory of special libraries, Japan) (Tokyo: Senmon Toshokan Kyōgikai, 1969– [published every three years]), and *Zenkoku toshokan annai: hoi: bunshokan shiryōkan hakubutsukan o chushin ni*, edited by Shoshi Kenkyū Konwakai (Tokyo: San'ichi Shobo [frequently revised]). Remember that reference services and interlibrary loan services are not yet widespread. It is wise, therefore, to make a thorough search within this country for the materials you need before you take a trip to Japan. As of June 1992, there were over 3.6 million volumes of Japanese books and over 8,000 titles of serials available in the United States. Naomi Fukuda's *Survey of Japanese Collections in the United States, 1979–1980* (Michigan Papers in Japanese Studies 4) (Ann Arbor: Center for Japanese Studies, University of Michigan, 1981; ix, 180p.) is still of great value for searching materials in American libraries.

Chapter Thirteen
A Final Note

When you decide on a topic for your master's essay or an extensive research paper, you need to do a bibliographic search for theses written in the past and for other research done in the field. When you undertake a Ph.D. dissertation, for example, it is an absolute necessity to find out what has been published on your topic. If you neglect this step, duplication of work is possible, and it is hard to conduct original research. If you want to write a paper on "the author's view of nature in *Tsurezuregusa* 徒然草," you might not be expected to write a completely original paper on this subject, but the first thing you should ask is, "Is there anything written on *Tsurezuregusa*?" This is your first step.

A list of books and articles on a subject is called a bibliography. Is there such a list in Japanese literature? A list of listings of books and articles on certain subjects is called a "bibliography of bibliographies." The most important list in Japanese that functions as a bibliography of bibliographies is *Nihon no sankō tosho: Kaisetsu sōran* (V-3). When you check this source, you will be able to find information on what kind of lists are available in what subject areas, with an explanation, called an annotation, under each entry. For *Tsurezuregusa* check the section for literature. In the literature section, you will find lists on various topics in Japanese literature. You can choose the ones you think might be useful to you, and, if you are lucky, you will find them in your library.

To find out what books have been published on a certain subject, check *Nihon zenkoku shoshi* (I-24), which is a national bibliography of Japan compiled by the National Diet Library. This weekly publication has an annual cumulative volume. It continues *Zen Nihon shuppanbutsu sōmokuroku* (I-22), which continued the catalogs of the National Diet Library (I-19/21) and *Kokuritsu Kokkai Toshokan shozō Meijiki kankō tosho mokuroku* (I-18). The national bibliographies of Japan that cover the period prior to these works are *Kokusho sōmokuroku* (I-16) and *Kotenseki sōgō mokuroku* (I-17), which cover pre-Meiji publications.

By going through these national bibliographies, you can find many books on *Tsurezuregusa*. If the paper you are writing is a short and simple one, you may stop your bibliographic search at this point. But for a serious thesis or research paper, you need to go further. This search is incomplete because materials that are not in book format, such as articles that appeared in journals, cannot be found by a search through library catalogs.

Journal articles are more important than books, particularly in the field of science and technology. Even in the humanities, bulletins and reports of universities and research institutes cannot be neglected. You need to search a listing of journal articles by subject, which is generally called a periodical index. The most important one is *Zasshi kiji sakuin* (II-1). By checking this, you should be able to find material on *Tsurezuregusa* that appeared in formats other than books. By conducting this search, you can comprehend the recent trends in research, how topics concerning *Tsurezuregusa* have been treated, or the depth of the research. This listing goes back only to 1948, when the newly established National Diet Library started its work. It is also necessary to use other sources in the specific field. For example, in the field of Japanese literature you should refer to *Kokubungaku nenkan* (X-24) for a more recent and exhaustive bibliography. By using its predecessors, such as *Kokubungaku kenkyū bunken mokuroku*, along with other bibliographies in the field of Japanese literature, you can search journal articles up to the early Meiji period and thus conduct a systematic retrospective search of materials related to *Tsurezuregusa*.

In an actual situation, you will use special bibliographies in your subject area first, such as *Kokubungaku nenkan* or a *Tsurezuregusa shoshi* if there is any, then search general bibliographies such as *Zasshi kiji sakuin*, which include extensive information on various topics, as a supplement to the former. And it is important to know the strengths and weaknesses of each bibliography, not just its general characteristics. If you are not aware of the strengths and weaknesses of the bibliographic tool you use, your search might be time-consuming and ineffective.

In the field of humanities and social sciences, the number of listings you have to go through rarely exceeds twenty. It is thus imperative to have a good overview of the subject area, to know the strengths and weaknesses of each tool, and to use them to supplement each other.

An evaluation of each bibliography usually can be done by judging the quality of the *hanrei*, the instructions of how to use the book, and by looking at the table of contents. The reliability of a bibliography can also be evaluated from the name-value of its author and publisher; from the coverage of the bibliography, for example, whether the bibliography includes journal articles or books; from its depth, that is, whether it is a simple inclusive listing or an evaluative bibliography; and from the period of coverage. By knowing these facts, you will be able to use the bibliography effectively and to judge whether to search for more recent publications

Now that you know what type of bibliographies are available on *Tsurezuregusa*, the next step is to find out where the materials are held. If your library does not own the items you need, you must use catalogs that have a different function from bibliographies in the strict sense of the word. They are the tools for finding out where the materials you need are located. In the United States, you can use *National Union Catalog* or published catalogs of the major East Asian collections, if your library does not have a computer terminal for on-line catalogs such as RLIN-CJK or OCLC-CJK. In Japan there is no nationwide list for this type of material published after 1868, so unless you have access to NACSIS Union Catalog Databases (156 participating libraries; data regarding 500 million Japanese and foreign books as of March 1991), you will have to check individual libraries. When the National Diet Library's records are added to NACSIS Union Catalog Databases, and more libraries participate, this will become a very useful on-line catalog for Japan.

For journals in the United States, use the *Union List of Serials in Libraries of the United States and Canada* (IV-3) and *New Serials Titles* (IV-4), and for Japanese-language journals in the United States and Canada held in East Asian collections, use the *National Union List of Current Japanese Serials in East Asian Libraries of North America* (IV-5). There is a union list besides *Kokuritsu Kokkai Toshokan shozō kokunai chikuji kankōbutsu mokuroku* (IV-6) in Japan. In *Gakujutsu zasshi sōgō mokuroku* (IV-7) you will be able to find detailed information on the journal holdings of Japanese academic libraries. After you find out which libraries hold the issue of the journal you need, you can use the interlibrary loan service, ask for a photocopy, or go to that library in person to use the materials.

If you find a book and wish to purchase it, you need to check the availability of the item. If it is a recent publication, you might check *Shuppan nenkan* (III-1) which is the annual listing of Japanese publications. But for checking availability, it is better to consult *Nihon shoseki sōmokuroku* (III-2) because it also contains information about the price and the publisher. For journals, consult *Nihon zasshi sōran*, which is the journal counterpart to *Shuppan nenkan*. It can be used to verify information and to order, but it does not provide the availability of issues of journals that have already been published. Usually, journal articles are obtained through photocopying.

After going through these steps, you should be able to obtain the materials you need for your paper. This process requires much time and patience, so allow enough time and start early.

You will be better off if you begin your research on a wider topic than you might actually write about, and do the systematic bibliographic search according to the process we have discussed above. Then, you will not have to redo your search if you should find that your topic is too narrow and nothing has been written on it. Finally, good luck in your search!

Subject Index

acquiring research materials, by bibliographic search, 131–32; books, 40–42; journal articles, 42–43
ALA. See American Library Association
American Library Association (ALA), 39
atlases, 101–2
azana, 54

bibliographic databases. See specific databases
bibliographic entry, sample, 138–39
bibliographic search, retrospective, 10–11; steps, 40–45, 142–45
bibliographies, annotated, 13–14, 48, 137; of atlases, 102; of biographies, 69–72; of books on Japan, 12–13; compiling, 137; coverage of, 137; of dissertations, 13–14, 21–22; general, 9–24; of individuals, 69–70; of Japanese-language materials, 16–22; of journals, 42–44; of maps, 101–2; national, 16–21, 40; personal, 69–70; of reference works, 47–48; retrospective, 10–22; of series, 35; subject, 115; of translations, 15–16, 124–25; universal, 40–42; of Western-language materials, 9–16; see also Japanese literature, bibliographies of
biographies, 61–68; bibliographies of, 69–72; of Westerners, 65
BIPS, 32
books in print, Japanese, 33–34
bookstores, 35

buying books for personal use, 35

calendars, 104–8; Gregorian, 104; lunar, 105; solar, 105
calendrical conversion tables, 105–8
Cataloging in Publication (CIP), 20
cataloging rules. See Nippon Cataloging Rules
catalogs, of books, 32–35; library, 39–46; of periodicals, 36–37; of publishers, 32–38; of serials, 42–43; of serials in East Asian libraries in the U.S.A., 41; see also bibliographies, national
CBI, 32–33
CD-HIASK, 29–30
Center for Research Libraries (CRL), 43
chronological conversion tables, 106
chronologies, 108–11; see also Japanese literature, chronologies of
CIP. See Cataloging in Publication
citation of sources, 136–39
classification systems. See Dewey Decimal Classification; Library of Congress, card catalog; Nippon Decimal Classification
collected works, finding contents of, 35, 116–23
CONSER. See Cooperative On-line Serials Program
Cooperative On-line Serials Program, 42, 42n.4
CRL. See Center for Research Libraries
CULCON. See U.S.-Japan Conference on Cultural and Educational Interchange

146

SUBJECT INDEX 147

cycle, sexagenary (sixty-year). *See eto*

dakuon, 139
databases. *See* specific databases
dates, conversion of, 105–6
DDC. *See* Dewey Decimal Classification
Dewey Decimal Classification (DDC), 33
diacritical marks, 138
dictionaries, 76–92; accent, 88; of archaic words, 87; of argots, 88; bilingual, 76–77; biographical, 61–65; of Chinese characters, 76–84; Chinese-Japanese, 76–84; of classical Japanese, 87; of dialects, 88; of difficult readings, 81; etymological, 91; of fables and phrases, 81, 91–92; of first names, 63; Japanese-English, 76, 83; Japanese-Japanese, 84–92; *Kan-Wa*, 76–84; *kokugo*, 84-92; of loanwords, 87–88; of new words, 87; of onomatopoeias, 90, 91; pronunciation, 88; of proverbs, 92; reversed word order, 81, 82, 86; of slang, 88; of specific periods, 87; of synonyms, 88, 89, 91; thesaurus, 88, 91
directories, of government officials, 59; of libraries, 140–41; of researchers, 59, 61; of research institutions, 140
dissertations. *See* doctoral dissertations
doctoral dissertations, in Japanese, 21-22; in Western languages, 13–14

encyclopedias, 92–95; English on Japan, 93; pre-Meiji, 93; of specific fields, 93, 95; *see also* Japanese literature, encyclopedias of
eras, calendrical. *See nengō*
eto, 106–10
etymologies. *See* dictionaries, etymological

filing rules, 39, 39n.1, 136–39

gagō. *See* names, alternate
Gakujutsu Jōhō Sentaa, 41, 43, 140, 144
gazetteers, 98–102
geimei. *See* names, alternate
genealogies, 68–69
gengō. *See nengō*
geography. *See* names, geographical; gazetteers
ginengō. *See nengō*, private
gō. *See* names, alternate
gyakubiki jiten. *See* dictionaries, reversed word order

hakusho, 95
han, 137
hanrei, 17, 144
hen, 83
Hepburn system. *See* romanization
historical atlases, 101–2
hyakka nenkan, 95
Hyakumantō darani, 2–3

indexes, 25–31; of collected works, 116; of essays, 116; of geographical names, 99; of literary works, 116, 119; of newspaper articles, 29–30; of journal articles, 25–29, 143; of personal names, 65–68; of poetry, 123
interlibrary loan, 41, 45, 140
International Standard Book Number (ISBN), 32
ISBN. *See* International Standard Book Number

Japanese collections in the United States, 131, 141, 144
Japanese libraries, 131, 140–41
Japanese literature, 115–35; basic research materials for, 128–32; bibliographies of, 115–16, 128–29; bibliographies of authors of, 130–31; biographical dictionaries of, 127; chronologies of, 126; collection of articles in *kiyō*, 132, 132n.1; dictionaries of, 126–27; encyclopedias of, 126–27;

handbooks on, 127; history of, 126; history of the study of, 128; indexes to classics, 116; to essays, 116–19; to individual works, 115–20; to information on authors, 130–31; to journal articles, 128–29; to monographic series, 116; to poems, 120, 123; to *tanka*, 120, 122–23; library collections of, 131–32; manuscripts of, 16–19, 41; readings of titles, 120; selective bibliographies of, 130–31; translations of, 124–25; trends in the study of, 128–29; yearbooks of, 120, 128
Japanese studies, history of, 4–8
Japan-MARC, 20
J-BISC (Japan Biblio-Disc), 20
jikkan. See eto
JIS *kanji* (Japan Industrial Standard Characters), 79
journals. *See* bibliographies, of journals
jūbakoyomi, 52; *see also* dictionaries, of difficult readings; Japanese literature, readings of titles; names, readings and writings of
jūnishi. See eto

kabane, 52–53
kaidai. See bibliographies, annotated
kaigen. See nengō
kan (bibliographic unit), 137
kanazukai, 79, 138, 138n.1
Kan-Wa jiten, 76–84
kigen. See nengō
kiyō, 132, 132n.1
kōki, 105
Kokubungaku Kenkyū Shiryōkan, 129, 140
kokugo jiten. See dictionaries, *kokugo*
kokuji, 77, 81
Kokuritsu Kokkai Toshokan (National Diet Library, NDL), 1, 12, 18, 19, 20, 21, 28, 41, 45, 57, 70, 142, 143, 144
kun, 77
kunrei-shiki. See romanization
kutōten, 139

libraries, East Asian. *See* Japanese collections in the United States
libraries, Japanese, 140–41
library catalogs, 39–46
library guidebooks. *See* libraries, Japanese
library networks. *See* Gakujutsu Jōhō Sentaa; Online Computer Library Center (OCLC); and Research Libraries Information Network (RLIN)
Library of Congress, 6, 20, 40, 41, 43, 138, card catalog, 40; card number, 32
literary works. *See* Japanese literature
loanwords. *See* dictionaries, of loanwords
locating, books when author unknown, 119, 123; books when title unknown, 119; individual literary works in a collection, 35, 116, 118–23; poems, 123; poems from fragments, 120

macron, 138, 139
maki. See kan
maps. *see* bibliographies, of maps
memoirs. *See kiyō*
myōji taitō, 53

NACSIS. *See* Gakujutsu Jōhō Sentaa
names, aliases, 54; alternate, 54–55; of foreigners written in *kanji*, 56; geographical, 98–102; personal, 52–75; readings and writings, 55–57, 59, 66; surnames, 53–54; written in *kana*, 56; *see also yōmei*
national bibliographies. *See* bibliographies, national
National Center for Science Information System (NACSIS). *See* Gakujutsu Jōhō Sentaa
National Diet Library (NDL). *See* Kokuritsu Kokkai Toshokan
NCR. *See* Nippon Cataloging Rules
NDC. *See* Nippon Decimal Classification

NDL. *See* Kokuritsu Kokkai Toshokan
nengō, 104–11; private, 104; unofficial, 104
nenkan. *See* yearbooks
nenpyō. *See* chronologies
newspapers, directories of publishers of, 36; holding lists, 42; indexes, 29–30; reduced-size editions, 30; yearbooks, 30, 95
Nihon Kindai Bungakukan, 140
Nihon-shiki. *See* romanization
Nikkei TELECOM, 29
Nippon Cataloging Rules (NCR), 139, 139n.2
Nippon Decimal Classification (NDC), 33, 33n.2

OCLC. *See* Online Computer Library Center
OCLC-CJK, 40, 40n.2, 45, 131, 144
on, 77
Online Computer Library Center (OCLC), 40, 40n.1
online databases, of books in Japanese, 29–30, 40; of serials, 42, 42n.4
ordering books. *See* acquiring research materials, books

pen name. *See* names, alternate
periodicals, directories of, 36–37; holding lists of, 42–43; indexes to articles in, 25–29
personal bibliographies. *See* bibliographies, personal
personal names. *See* names, personal
place-names. *See* gazetteers; names, geographical
poems. *See* Japanese literature, indexes to poems; locating, poems
preface date, 137
printing, history of Japanese, 2–4
pronunciation. *See* dictionaries, pronunciation
proverbs. *See* dictionaries, of fables and phrases; of proverbs
pseudonyms. *See* names, alternate
publications, availability of, 33–34; numbers of, 1, 33; of Meiji period, 19; pre-Meiji, 2–4; of Japanese publishers, 1
publishers' catalogs, 32–38; of books, 32–35; of serials, 36–37
publishing, history of, 2–4, 18

reference works, guides to, 47–51
rekishiteki kanazukai. *See* kanazukai
research, procedures for conducting, 43–45, 115, 142–45
Research Libraries Information Network (RLIN), 40, 40n.1
RLIN. *See* Research Libraries Information Network
RLIN-CJK, 40, 40n.1, 45, 131, 144
romanization, 137–38
ryakuji, 81

seion, 139
series, monographic, contents of, 35, 116
sexagenary cycles. *See* eto
shinengō. *See* nengō, private
shukusatsuban. *See* newspapers, reduced-size editions
sokuon, 139
statistics, 95
studio names. *See* names, alternate
style manuals, 136
subject bibliographies, 115
surnames. *See* names, surnames
synonyms. *See* dictionaries, of synonyms

technicalities of style, 136–39
ten stems. *See* eto
thesaurus, 88–89
times of day, 108–9
trade catalogs. *See* catalogs, of publishers
translations. *See* bibliographies, of translations; Japanese literature, translations of
tsukuri, 83
tsūshō. *See* names, alternate

uji, 53

union catalogs. *See* catalogs, library
union list of periodicals. *See* catalogs, library
U.S.-Japan Conference on Cultural and Educational Interchange, 7

varifying information, 43–44; of personal names, 57–61

who's who, 58-61

word division, 138

yearbooks; encyclopedias, 95; of newspaper publishers', 30, 95; statistics, 95
yōmei, 54
yōon, 139
yutōyomi, 52

zodiac signs, 106

Title Index

Asahi nenkan, 30, 59, 95
Asahi Shinbun gendai yōgo Chiezō, 87
Asahi Shinbun kiji sōran, 30
Asahi Shinbun shukusatsuban, 30

Basic Japanese-English dictionary, 76
Bibliographie japonaise, 10, 13
Bibliographie japonaise ou catalogue des ouvrages relatifs au Japon qui ont 'et'e publie's depuis le XVe sie'cle jusqu'a' nos jours. *See* Bibliographie japonaise
Bibliographie von Japan, 10, 11, 13
Bibliography of Asian Studies, 10–12, 13
Bibliography of Reference Works for Japanese Studies, 48, 95
Bibliography of the Japanese Empire, 10, 13
Biographical Dictionary of Japanese History, 64, 127
Biographical Dictionary of Japanese Literature, 64, 127
Books in Print, 32, 33, 34
Bulletin of Far Eastern Bibliography, 10, 11
Bungei nenkan, 120
Bunkajin meiroku, 59

Catalog of Materials on Japan in Western Languages in the National Diet Library Formerly in the Collection of the Ueno Library, 1872–1960, 12–13
Catalog of Materials on Japan in Western Languages in the National Diet Library, 1948–1975, 13
Catalog of Materials on Japan in Western Languages in the National Diet Library, 1976–1986, 13
Catalogue of Books in English on Japan 1945–1981, 12
Catalogue of Books on Japan Translated from the Japanese into English, 16
CBI. *See* Cumulative Book Index
Chicago Manual of Style, The, 136
Chiezō. *See* Asahi Shinbun gendai yōgo Chiezō
Chihōshi bunken sōgō mokuroku, 102
Chimei yomikata jiten, 99
Chosakuken daichō: Bunkajin meiroku, 59
Chū-Nichi-Ō taishō sekai chimei jinmei jiten, 56, 99
Cumulative Bibliography of Asian Studies, 10, 11–12, 13
Cumulative Book Index (CBI), 32–33

Daibukan, 59
Daijinmei jiten, 57, 61, 63
Daijiten, 81, 83
Dai Kangorin, 79
Dai Kangorin goi sōran, 79
Dai Kan-Wa jiten, 77–79, 81, 83
Dai Kan-Wa jiten goi sakuin, 79
Dai Nihon bunken chizu, 102
Dai Nihon chimei jisho, 99, 101
Dai Nihon dokushi chizu, 101

151

TITLE INDEX

Dai Nihon josei jinmei jisho, 64
Dai Nihon kokugo jiten, 86
Denki hyōden zenjōhō 45/89, 70
Dictionary of Japanese Artists, A, 64
Dissertation Abstracts International, 14
Doctoral Dissertations on Asia: An Annotated Bibliographical Journal of Current International Research, 14
Doctoral Dissertations on Japan and Korea, 1969–1979: An Annotated Bibliography of Studies in Western Languages, 14

Edogo daijiten, 87
Engeki hyakka daijiten, 64, 93

Gakujutsu zasshi sōgō mokuroku: Wabun hen, 43, 44, 132, 140, 144
Gendai bukkosha jiten 1980–1982, 64
Gendai bungaku kenkyū: Jōhō to shiryō, 130
Gendai Nihon bungaku nenpyō, 111
Gendai Nihon bungaku sōran shiriizu, 116, 118, 119, 123
Gendai Nihon chimei yomikata daijiten, 98–100
Gendai Nihongo hōgen daijiten, 88
Gendai Nihon jinmeiroku, 58
Gendai Nihon shakai, 35
Gendai Nihon shippitsusha daijiten, 57, 58, 59
Gendai yōgo no kiso chishiki, 87
Genshoku zuten Nihon bijutsushi nenpyō, 111, 112
Giseigo gitaigo kan'yōku jiten, 90–91
Guide to Reference Books, 26, 47–48
Guide to Reference Books for Japanese Studies, A, 48
Gunsho keizubushū, 69
Gunsho ruijū, 69, 116
Gyakubiki jukugorin, 86
Gyakubiki Kōjien, 86

Hon'yaku tosho mokuroku, 124
Hōreki seireki taishōhyō, 105, 106
Humanities Index, 26

Index translationum: International Bibliography of Translations, 15–16

Ingo jiten, 88
International Index, 26
Introductory Bibliography for Japanese Studies, An, 15, 16
Iwanami kogo jiten, 87
Iwanami Seiyō jinmei jiten, 65

Japan and Korea: An Annotated Bibliography of Doctoral Dissertations in Western Languages, 1877–1969, 13–14
Japanese Literature in European Languages: A Bibliography, 124–25
Japanese Literature in Foreign Languages 1945–1990, 16, 124–25
Japanese Names: A Comprehensive Index by Characters and Readings, 55
Japanese National Bibliography, 20
Japanese Periodicals and Newspapers in Western Languages: An International Union List, 42, 131
Japanese Publications in Foreign Languages 1945–1990, 16
Japan Who Was Who: Bukkosha Jiten 1983–1987, 64
Jidaibetsu kokugo daijiten, 87
Jiji nenkan, 30
Jinbutsu bunken sakuin, 70
Jinbutsu refarensu jiten, 57, 65–67
Jinbutsu shoshi sakuin, 69–70
Jinbutsu shoshi taikei, 70
Jinbutsu sōsho, 68
Jinji kōshinroku, 58, 60
Jinmei yomikata jiten, 56
Jōhō chishiki imidas, 87

Kadokawa gairaigo jiten, 87–88
Kadokawa kogo daijiten, 87
Kadokawa Nihon chimei daijiten, 101
Kadokawa ruigo shinjiten, 88–89, 91
Kan-Ei jukugo ribaasu jiten, 81, 82
Kansei chōshū shokafu, 69
Kan'yaku Kanmei Seiyō jinmei jiten, 56
Keizu bunken shiryō sōran, 69
Keizu kenkyū no kiso chishiki: Kakei ni miru Nihon no rekishi, 69
Kenkyūsha kenkyū kadai sōran:

Jinbun shakai kagaku hen, 59, 61, 62
Kenkyusha's New Japanese-English Dictionary, 137
Kihon gairaigo jiten, 88
Kindai Nihon sōgō nenpyō, 110
Kindai sakka kenkyū jiten, 130
Kodansha Encyclopedia of Japan, The, 64, 93, 138n.1
Kojin zenshū naiyō sōran, 119
Kojin zenshū sakuhinmei sōran, 119
Koji ruien, 93, 94
Koji seigo meigen daijiten, 92
Koji zokushin kotowaza daijiten, 92
Kō Kan-Wa jiten, 79, 80, 83
Kokubungaku kenkyū bunken mokuroku, 129
Kokubungaku kenkyū bunken mokuroku: Shōwa 16-nen-Shōwa 37-nen, 129
Kokubungaku Kenkyū Shiryōkanzō chikuji kankōbutsu mokuroku, 131–32
Kokubungaku kenkyū shomoku kaidai, 130
Kokubungaku nenjibetsu ronbunshū, 132
Kokubungaku nenkan, 28, 129, 143
Kokugo kokubun, 129
Kokugo kokubungaku kenkyū bunken mokuroku, 1963–1970, 129, 143
Kokugo kokubungaku nenkan, 128, 129
Kokugo kokubun kenkyū zasshi sakuin, 128
Kokuritsu Kokkai Toshokan choshamei tenkyoroku: Meiji ikō Nihon jinmei, 57
Kokuritsu Kokkai Toshokan shozō chizu mokuroku, 102
Kokuritsu Kokkai Toshokan shozō hakushi ronbun mokuroku, 21–22
Kokuritsu Kokkai Toshokan shozō kokunai chikuji kankōbutsu mokuroku, 37, 43, 132, 144
Kokuritsu Kokkai Toshokan shozō Meijiki kankō tosho mokuroku, 19, 20, 142
Kokuritsu Kokkai Toshokan shozō wazasshi mokuroku, 43
Kokuritsu Kokkai Toshokan zōsho mokuroku, 20, 140
Kokusho sōmokuroku, 16–18, 41, 115, 116, 140, 143
Kotenseki sōgō mokuroku, 16–19, 41, 143
Kōwa tsūreki, 106
Kōza Nihon bungaku, 131
Kugyō bunin, 59

Library of Congress Cataloging Service Bulletin, 138
Library of Congress Catalogs, 40
List of Foreign Literary Works Translated into Japanese, A, 124

Mainichi nenkan, 30, 95
Manual for Writers of Term Papers, Theses, and Dissertations, A, 136
Meiji kakochō: Bukko jinmei jiten shinteiban, 63
Meiji nyūsu jiten, 30
Meiji Taishō Shōwa hon'yaku bungaku mokuroku, 124
Meiji Taishō Shōwa sakka kenkyū daijiten, 130
MLA Handbook for Writers of Research Papers, Theses, and Dissertations, 136
Modern Japanese Literature in Translation: A Bibliography, 124–125
Modern Reader's Japanese-English Character Dictionary, 76

Namae kara hiku jinmei jiten, 63
Nankun jiten, 81
National Union Catalog (NUC), 40–41, 44, 45, 131, 140, 144
National Union List of Japanese Serials in Current East Asian Libraries of North America, 42–43, 131, 144
Nenkan hakusho zenjōhō 45/89, 37
Nenkan jinbutsu bunken mokuroku, 70, 71
Nenpyō Nihon rekishi, 108
New Japanese-English Character Dictionary, 83
New Serial Titles, 42, 131, 144

154 TITLE INDEX

New York Times Index: A Book of Record, 29
Nihon bungaku daijiten, 70, 126, 127
Nihon bungaku dainenpyō, 111, 126
Nihon bungaku kenkyū bunken yōran, 129
Nihon bungaku kenkyū shiryō sōsho, 130–31
Nihon bungaku sakuhinmei yomikata jiten, 120, 121
Nihon bungaku zenshi, 126
Nihon bunka sōgō nenpyō, 110–11
Nihon bunken chizu chimei sōran, 102
Nihon chimei sakuin, 99
Nihon choshamei sōmokuroku, 41, 57
Nihongo daijiten, 84–86
Nihongo gogen jiten, 91
Nihongo hatsuon akusento jiten, 88
Nihon hakushi gakuiroku, 21–22
Nihon hakushi gakui ronbun sakuin, 21–22
Nihon hakushiroku, 21–22
Nihon hōgen daijiten, 88
Nihon in'yō rekijitsu taishōhyō, 106
Nihon jinbutsu bunken mokuroku, 69, 70
Nihon jinmei daijiten, 57, 61, 63, 65
Nihon jinmei jiten, 63
Nihon jinmei tenkyoroku, 57, 66
Nihonjin no jiden, 68
Nihon josei jinmei jiten, 64
Nihon keifu sōran, 69
Nihon kenkyū no tame no sankō tosho. See Guide to Reference Books for Japanese Studies, A
Nihon Kindai Bungaku daijiten, 64, 127
Nihon Kindai Bungakukan shozō shuyō zasshi mokuroku, 132
Nihon kokugo daijiten, 83, 84, 85, 86, 91
Nihon koten bungaku daijiten, 126–127
Nihon mokuroku kisoku, 139n.2
Nihon nenkan sōran, 37
Nihon no myōji, 55
Nihon no sankō tosho: Kaisetsu sōran, 28, 48, 49, 50, 64, 92, 93, 130, 142
Nihon no sankō tosho: Shikiban, 48
Nihon no shiika zenjōhō 27/90, 123
Nihon no shōsetsu zenjōhō 27/90, 119
Nihon rekijitsu genten, 106
Nihonreki seireki gappi taishōhyō, 106, 107
Nihon rekishi chimei taikei, 99, 101
Nihon rekishi chizu, 101–2
Nihon rekishi daijiten, 102, 108
Nihon rekishi nenpyō, 108
Nihon seishi daijiten, 55
Nihon shinbun zasshi benran, 36
Nihon shi nenpyō, 110
Nihon shinshiroku, 58
Nihon shoseki sōmokuroku, 1, 2, 33–34, 35, 145
Nihon sōsho sakuin, 116
Nihon tōkei nenkan, 95
Nihon zasshi sōran, 1, 36, 145
Nihon zenkoku shoshi, 20, 21, 33, 34, 35, 44, 142
Nihon zenkoku shoshi shūkanban, 20, 21, 115
Nihon zuihitsu sakuin, 116
Nihon zuihitsu taisei, 116
NUC. See National Union Catalog

Ōya Sōichi Bunko zasshi kiji sakuin sōmokuroku, 28

Paperbound Books in Print, 32
Princeton Companion to Classical Japanese Literature, The, 127

Rainichi Seiyō jinmei jiten, 65
Reader's Guide to Periodical Literature, 25
Rekishi jinmei yomikata jiten, 56
Research in Japanese Sources: A Guide, 52n.1, 136

Sakuhinmei kara hikeru Nihon bungaku hyōron, shisōka kojin zenshū annai, 119
Sakuhinmei kara hikeru Nihon bungaku sakka, shōsetsuka, kojin zenshū annai, 119
Sakuhinmei kara hikeru Nihon bungaku shiika, haijin kojin

zenshū annai, 123
Sakuhinmei kara hikeru Nihon bungaku zenshū annai, 119
Sankei Nihon shinshi nenkan, 58
Sansei sōran, 106
Seigorin: Koji kotowaza kan'yōku, 92
Seishi kakei daijiten, 68
Seiyō jinbutsu refarensu jiten, 66
Seiyō jinmei yomikata jiten, 56
Sekai daihyakka jiten, 70, 92
Selected List of Books and Articles on Japan in English, French and German, A, 12
Senmon jōhō kikan sōran, 140
Shiika zenshū, 123
Shiika zenshū sakkamei sōran, 123
Shiika zenshū sakuhinmei sōran, 123
Shiika zenshu shiika naiyō sōran, 123
Shinbun shūsei Meiji hennenshi, 30
Shinbun shūsei Shōwa hennenshi, 30
Shinbun shūsei Taishō hennenshi, 30
Shin Daijiten, 81
Shin Kan-Ei jiten, 81, 83
Shin Nihon bunken chizu, 102
Shinpen Kokka taikan, 120, 122
Shokuinroku, 59
Shoshi nenkan, 48, 50
Shōwa bukko jinmeiroku 1926–1979, 64
Shōwa nyūsu jiten, 30
Shūkanshi indekkusu, 28
Shūkanshi kiji sakuin 81/87, 28
Shuppan nenkan, 1, 33, 34, 35, 145
Shuppan nyūsu, 33
Social Sciences and Humanities Index, 26
Social Sciences Index, 26
Sōgōshi indekkusu, 28
Sōgōshi kiji sakuin 81/87, 28
Sonpi bunmyaku, 69
Survey of Japanese Collections in the United States, 1979–1980, 141

Taishō kakochō: Bukko jinmei jiten, 63–64
Taishō nyūsu jiten, 30
Teikoku Toshokan Kokuritsu Toshokan Wakan tosho bunrui mokuroku, 19–20
Teikoku Toshokan Wakan tosho shomei mokuroku, 19, 20
Tōyō jinbutsu refarensu jiten, 66

Ulrich's International Periodicals Directory, 36
Union List of Serials in Libraries of the United States and Canada, 42, 131, 144

Walford's Guide to Reference Materials, 26, 48
Wamyō ruijushō, 101
Watakushi no rirekisho, 68
Who's Who in Japan, 58

Yomiuri nenkan, 30
Yomiuri nyūsu sōran: Nyūsu kiji no sakuin to shōroku, 30

Zasshi kiji sakuin: Jinbun shakai hen, 26–27, 28, 143
Zasshi kiji sakuin: Jinbun shakai hen. Ruiseki sakuinban, 26–27, 28, 129
Zasshi shinbun sōkatarogu, 36
Zenkoku tokushu korekushon yōran, 140
Zenkoku toshokan annai: hoi, 140
Zen Nihon shuppanbutsu sōmokuroku, 20, 21, 142
Zenshū naiyō sōran, 116
Zenshū sakkamei sōran, 119
Zenshū sakuhinmei sōran, 119
Zenshū sōgō mokuroku, 35
Zenshū sōsho saimoku sōran, 116, 117
Zōho kokugo kokubungaku kenkyūshi taisei, 128

CPSIA information can be obtained at www.ICGtesting.com
Printed in the USA
BVOW080002270613

324414BV00001B/27/P